PRAISE FOR

THE MONEY & MEANING

"Many of us can lose sight of the fact that money is a tool to support our values, not create them. Jeff's book is a reminder that while having the tools to make smart financial decisions is important, distinguishing 'the deeper needs of the spirit from the superficial demands of the ego' is what will lead us to live lives without regret."

Ross Levin, CFP®
Founder, Accredited Investors Wealth Management; Author,
The Wealth Management Index

"At Halftime, when we work with individuals to help them find and live out their calling, we often talk about two journeys. One is the journey in your head; the other is the journey in your heart. In this book, Jeff does a great job of addressing both. To me, that's the key to an abundant life. The head journey guides what you do and how you do it. The heart journey helps you know why you are doing what you are doing. One is more practical; the other involves soul-level work. *The Money and Meaning Journey* expounds the two tracks in a way that both equips and motivates the reader."

Tom McGehee
Co-Executive Director, Halftime Institute

"A rare combination of heart and reason; Jeff does a fantastic job of defining the hero's journey and how we are all the heroes in our own story."

Daniel Crosby, PhD
Chief Behavioral Officer, Orion Advisor Solutions

"If you are planning for retirement, Jeff's book importantly provides both a financial and life roadmap, along with a highly relatable memoir, making it a worthy companion to Alan Spector and Keith Lawrence's *Your Retirement Quest*."

Larry Swedroe
Principal and Director of Research, Buckingham Strategic Wealth; Author, Your Complete Guide to a Successful and Secure Retirement

"A. W. Tozer, the wise thinker and brilliant theologian of the mid-twentieth century, once said, 'A message must be not only timeless but timely, speaking to his own generation.' Jeff accomplishes this in *The Money and Meaning Journey*. His disciplined research, clear writing style, and engaging storytelling make this book compelling. These pages contain practical words for those who desire to use money in a way that honors God and honors others. His life experiences, from being a banker's son to now being a financial manager, uniquely qualify him to pen these thoughts. If you're looking for a fresh read on money, go no further and be blessed!"

Boyd Bailey
President, National Christian Foundation (Georgia); President, Wisdom Hunters

"In this book, Jeff masterfully tells the reader what they've probably suspected all along: Reconciling personal finance and the pursuit of a meaningful life is hard to do. How can one live life unencumbered from financial worry when it seems the next market or economic catastrophe is just around the corner? Jeff shows us how in *The Money and Meaning Journey*. If it's not on your must-read list, it should be."

Rob Hoxton, CFP®, AIF®
Managing Member, Hoxton Planning & Management LLC;
Author, Think Ahead: Ten Reasons You Need a Financial Planner

"Thomas Merton is credited with proposing that 'People may spend their whole lives climbing the ladder of success only to find, once they reach the top, that the ladder is leaning against the wrong wall.' The essence of Jeff's book is to help keep readers from finding out too late that they've made a mistake with their ladder. Jeff's aim, expressed thoughtfully and clearly, is to help the reader to determine what's most important to them, then to guide them to make that a guiding star rather than an afterthought. Read his book, become wiser, and achieve your best life."

Larry Maddox
President, Horizon Wealth Advisors

"Countless authors through time have opined on the 'meaning of life' without acknowledging the role that wise financial planning plays in discovering this rare knowledge. By the same token, authors have filled volumes on maximizing returns, minimizing tax, and allocating risk without once conceding that financial success means little to those who lack self-awareness and inner fulfillment. In writing *The Money and Meaning Journey: A Guide to Clarity, Financial Confidence, and Joy*, Jeff Bernier strives to align these two concepts with the hope that readers might unearth life-altering joy on the way to earning financial success."

Daniel D. Munster, Esq.
The Eldercare & Special Needs Law Practice of Daniel D. Munster

"Jeff Bernier has written a book that is personal, practical, and inspirational. You will only want to read it if you are looking for a guide to a life well lived."

Mark Danzey
Executive Director, Narrow Gate: Equipping for Life

"This book provides sage advice on how to participate in evidenced-based investing to create a holistic plan, rather than trying to chase and time the market."

Eric Clarke
Chief Executive Officer, Orion Advisor Solutions

"Having read many financial planning books over the years, we found this book different in its content and approach ... refreshing. While the book offers plenty of 'blocking-and-tackling' know-how for wealth accumulation and management, the book makes a compelling case for expanding beyond just that and securing one's true mission in life. From the multiple messages and concepts offered in this book, the one that most resonated was that wealth and the joy of the journey can grow together."

Abe Rodriguez
Retired Director, Mexico, Caribbean, Central and Latin America, AT&T Mobility International

"Jeff Bernier's book takes a thoughtful, holistic approach. In it, he combines the fiduciary obligation to make investment decisions driven by what is in the reader's best interests with the wisdom that financial resources alone do not lead to happiness and a meaningful, purpose-driven life."

Robert C. Port
Partner, Gaslowitz Frankel LLC

"Each of us has a need placed in us to be significant and to find our uniquely designed purpose in life. The Bible has over twenty-six hundred passages on making financial decisions, so God knew this was going to be a major issue in every life. Jeff masterfully uses his life experiences as well as his search for true knowledge to assist the reader in clearly reprioritizing their lives around purpose and effective stewardship."

Bill Lohnes
President, Narrow Gate: Equipping for Life

"Knowing Jeff personally and professionally, I can tell you that this work is a refreshing read from a seasoned practitioner. He shares from his journey discovering the purpose of life and growing from the trappings of success. He not only offers sound money management advice but also helps others find joy in a life well lived."

Matthew Hendley

Generosity Ambassador/Relationship Manager, National Christian Foundation (Georgia)

"As a trusts and estates attorney, I have witnessed firsthand how the concepts in *The Money and Meaning Journey* can be implemented to help the reader define and attain not only their financial goals but also, very importantly, their *life* goals as well."

Kara C. Fleming, Esq.

The Law Office of Kara C. Fleming LLC

"Jeff's book outlines a liberating process for managing one's financial future that enables one to pursue their true interests. Following this robust, goal-focused, and planning-driven approach with the help of a guide has freed me to confidently enjoy my 'second act' rather than risk squandering it by worrying, making big mistakes, or attempting to amass the skills and resources of a competent financial advisor with a single client: myself."

Edwin J. Buckley Jr.

Retired President, Global Marketing, United Parcel Service

"Many of us view financial planning as all about money. We put our finances ahead of our purpose. Jeff helps to clarify that purpose determines our financial needs and strategies."

Lori Evers, CPA

Retired Certified Public Accountant; Chartered Advisor in Philanthropy; Consultant; Teacher; Mentor; Volunteer

"The author's wisdom gleaned from his personal life experiences coupled with a vast array of resources provides the reader with actionable steps for self-discovery as a basis for developing meaningful goals both financially and for personal well-being. This rare and refreshing guide allows a person to align their unique life focus with a financial approach that is balanced and realistic."

Norm and Linda

Retired Executives

"This book goes beyond teaching about replenishing financial reserves. Jeff also talks about replenishing our spiritual reserves. Taking time off and taking care of yourself are just as important as ensuring that you are financially secure for the rest of your life."

Matt Tanzy

Founder and Chief Executive Officer, 1st Payment Systems; Managing Director, Camp Lighthouse

"Jeff Bernier truly understands the purpose and greater meaning of money. His book can help authentically guide the reader to maximize the development and stewardship of their wealth. As a result, it can help them to clarify purpose and realize joy in their lives. Jeff offers invaluable insight to all of us through this book."

Ty Miller
Director of Sales (US), Attune Medical

"What a blessing to hear and see how Jeff has broken through to a second half having discovered the pearl of great price in this life: purpose working in tandem with joy! Sharing his journey and principles with all who read this book is a rich investment in helping others discover their purpose, pursue it with integrity, and live it out with both."

Steve Wood
Lead Pastor, Mount Pisgah Church

"In this book, Jeff brings to light that, although money is important, it's what you do with the money and finding your purpose that will give you a meaningful life. In my line of work, I see so many who have built their wealth and shift their focus to keeping it instead of finding the purpose behind the wealth. This book focuses on that: showing you how to live your best life."

Stephanie Franek
Partner, Stephanie Franek CPA LLC

"Jeff Bernier's timing is impeccable, once again! In *The Money and Meaning Journey*, Jeff uses his thirty-six-year track record to help you create the foundation for the life you want to live and the life you *could* live. It's not just smart investing; it's about creating the financial plan that supports the purpose of the life you are living rather than pushing your life into someone's else view of what you should do. With Jeff, your life is a spiritual journey.

"Jeff shares parts of his relatable journey—the challenging times, the sad times, the great times—and demonstrates how an integrated financial plan supported him every step of the way. And more importantly, if you desire to have an 'Act 2' in your life—where you can contribute more than you ever imagined—this book has you covered.

"Call it sage advice if you like, but make no mistake; the counsel in this book offers a partnership with your life's desires and is based entirely on evidence-based, time-tested financial strategy. And *please* pay special attention to the 'Six Financial Challenges' we *all* face and how to overcome them.

"In this book, Jeff helps you partner the God-given authenticity of your life's plan to the best financial strategies available."

Christopher "Chase" Carey, MBA
Third Degree Black Belt; President, CAREY Benefits

"I love the life stories and learnings Jeff Bernier provides in this book. By reading this book, one has the tools for a rewarding financial life and/or retirement."

Sam Maloy
Retired Sales Director, Eli Lilly

"Jeff walks us down a path of discovery to deeply understand ourselves and our own unique purposes in life, and he shows how we can take advantage of that understanding to create purpose, meaning, and satisfaction in the future chapters of our lives."

Terrence K. Quinn, JD

"Jeff articulates the importance of making a life plan and then an analytically based financial plan to support it."

Walter Mann
President, Zono Technologies

"*The Money and Meaning Journey* provides real financial tools to make wise decisions with what God has given us to steward, but it also engages the reader in a journey of personal discovery which connects wealth to joy on the bridge called 'purpose and calling.' Thanks, Jeff, for sharing your own story in a humble, authentic way, which encourages us all to realize who really owns what we possess."

Dick Gygi
Master Certified Coach, Halftime Institute of Nashville; Founder, Fuel For Good LLC

"Jeff Bernier thoughtfully lays out the importance of establishing 'what makes you come alive' and of deftly pairing those core pursuits with a long-term, fundamentals-driven investing approach. He emphasizes navigating these paths simultaneously, weaving journeys of the spirit with responsible planning of both one's circumstances and finances. Jeff shows how having the clarity and confidence of well-founded objectives, in combination with a pragmatic approach to markets, can alleviate much of the stress that often accompanies planning for life after retirement—encouraging readers to explore how wealth and purpose can grow together."

Dave Butler

Co-Chief Executive Officer and Dimensional Director,
Dimensional Fund Advisors

THE **MONEY & MEANING** JOURNEY

THE
MONEY &
MEANING
JOURNEY

A guide to clarity, financial confidence, and joy

JEFF BERNIER CFP®, CHFC, CFS

Advantage | Books

Published by Advantage, Charleston, South Carolina.
Member of Advantage Media.

ADVANTAGE is a registered trademark, and the Advantage colophon is a trademark of Advantage Media Group, Inc.

Printed in the United States of America.

10 9 8 7 6 5 4 3 2 1

ISBN: 978-1-64225-262-0 (Hardcover)
ISBN: 978-1-64225-436-5 (eBook)
LCCN: 2022914995

Book design by Analisa Smith.

Advantage Media helps busy entrepreneurs, CEOs, and leaders write and publish a book to grow their business and become the authority in their field. Advantage authors comprise an exclusive community of industry professionals, idea-makers, and thought leaders. Do you have a book idea or manuscript for consideration? We would love to hear from you at **AdvantageMedia.com**.

This book is dedicated to my parents, Walt and Beverly Bernier. I share parts of their story in this book. We are all influenced by our experiences. My mom taught me the value of relationships and putting others first. My dad demonstrated what it means to be loyal and how to serve clients and community with excellence. They both helped create the spiritual grounding that has served me well.

Contents

PART 1

Enjoying the Journey

CHAPTER 1

The Money and Meaning Journey

Don't ask what the world needs. Ask what
makes you come alive, and go do it.
Because what the world needs is people who have come alive.
—HOWARD THURMAN [1]

A Wonderful Life

If you've ever seen the perennial Christmas classic *It's a Wonderful Life*, you've met my father. No, I'm not a child of Hollywood, nor am I the son of Jimmy Stewart, the star of the film. I'm from Pelham, Georgia, with no connections to the movie industry. But my father is the real-life incarnation of George Bailey, the character Stewart made famous. Like Bailey, he was a much-beloved small-town banker who devoted his life to serving his local community. Like Bailey, my father

---

1 Howard Thurman, *The Living Wisdom of Howard Thurman: A Visionary for Our Time* (Louisville, Colorado: Sounds True, 2010).

took on his trusted leadership role as a young man following the death of his predecessor. And as with Bailey, my father's greatest joy was helping his customers solve their problems and achieve their goals.

I love my father, I'm proud of him, and throughout my life I've tried to emulate his example. But even the most noble lives are not always wonderful. Bailey must endure a dark night of the soul to fully appreciate his own good fortune. And I have learned as much from my father's sufferings and forbearance as I have from his triumphs and joys. Indeed, I can trace the genesis of this book back to his description of one of the darkest days in his life.

In 2003 my mother was diagnosed with cancer—the start of a two-year ordeal that preceded her death in 2005. Early on in her treatment, my father and I came home from the hospital following a surgery that had not gone as well as we'd hoped: we were now facing a dire prognosis and great uncertainty about her recovery. Deeply devoted to my mother, my father told me that this was one of the worst three days of his life. He then explained that he felt similarly bereft the day his own mother died. Because I now faced a similar possibility, I fully identified with his words. But what he said next shocked me. The final entry on his list—the sorrowful event he paired with an unsuccessful surgery and the death of his mother?

The day he retired.

Over the years that shock has gradually blossomed into an insight that shapes the core of this book. My father's purpose in life was all about taking care of the people in Pelham. That's a noble calling, and he excelled at it. Deprived of that purpose, however, his life lost much of its central meaning. *I knew* my father was much more than his job, but at some deep emotional level, maybe he did not. That he equated the suffering and death of loved ones with the loss of his job, that his happiness and fulfillment were in some complicated way tethered to his professional title, struck me as tragic.

My work as a financial advisor, however, has taught me that my father's anguish is far more prevalent than most of us realize. Again and again I see clients who've spent decades striving for success. They've built extraordinary careers and earned impressive titles and well-deserved accolades. Their kids are (finally!) showing their true potential. They've earned all the trappings of material success: a lovely home, a fancy car, a country club membership, and more. They *seem* to be living the American Dream.

But as they prepare for retirement or the second part of their lives, they find themselves—like my father—in a crisis they had not foreseen. "What trap is this? Where were its teeth concealed?" asks the poet Philip Larkin.[2] They've played by the rules, ticked off all the markers of achievement, yet their lives feel inexplicably empty. Echoing the famous words of a Jack Nicholson character, they ask, "Is this as good as it gets?"

Suddenly, their accomplishments and conquests simply aren't enough. They begin to feel like the child who, two weeks after Christmas, is already tired of all the new toys. This can be a challenging and confusing time. Just when they can finally relax a bit and bask in all they've achieved, they realize that external rewards no longer provide excitement and motivation. As a result, they catch themselves simply going through the motions, without the sense of joy they assumed would be an inevitable consequence of all their work.

Sound familiar?

That's because unless we make a conscious decision to lead a purpose-filled life, we may be destined to drift into these emotional

---

2   Philip Larkin, "Myxomatosis" in *Collected Poems* (London: Farrar, Straus and Giroux, 2004).

doldrums: stalled on a windless sea, our sails gone slack, our hope of new and exciting destinations replaced by feelings of frustration, boredom, and despair. We begin to lower our expectations or adopt a stoical resolve, resigning ourselves to what feels like our only possible fate. We see our old aspirations as outmoded or delusional and may look to fill our lives with mindless or even self-destructive diversions.

What was once "a wonderful life" seems drained of wonder. Our familiar energy becomes harder to find. As stress levels rise, we can even lose confidence in our abilities, develop negative attitudes, experience a decline in health, and settle into what Henry David Thoreau called "lives of quiet desperation." An urgent course correction is mandatory to avoid a classic midlife crisis filled with regret, burnout, and decline.

Second Acts

The novelist F. Scott Fitzgerald once famously said, "There are no second acts in American lives."[3] This book aims to refute that assertion.

In over thirty-six years of advising and coaching clients, I've found that many of us have either not found our purpose or, sadly, failed to pursue it because of financial worries.

In the chapters that follow, I'll help you recognize that your life is not a one-act play, and I'll serve as a guide to the stage management decisions you'll need to make so that Act 2, Act 3, Act 4, and so on can be the fulfillment of Act 1 rather than a dispiriting set of blank pages.

I believe we are all uniquely created by God with a purpose. I also believe that life is a journey to

---

3   F. Scott Fitzgerald, *The Last Tycoon* (New York: Scribner, 1995).

discover and pursue this God-inspired purpose. In over thirty-six years of advising and coaching clients, however, I've found that many of us have either not found our purpose or, sadly, failed to pursue it because of financial worries. My goal is to help you avoid that tragedy. How? First, by giving you the tools to discover what really matters in your life so you avoid the all-too-common pitfall of equating your higher purpose with your job title, your accomplishments, or your ego. Second, by clarifying how to make wealth management decisions aligned with those higher goals.

Many books explore questions of meaning and spiritual insight but ignore the financial planning that is a necessary condition for living in accord with your hard-won beliefs and insights. Conversely many other books provide valuable information about managing your money without ever considering the larger questions of what you intend to do with it or how much is enough. My experience has taught me that unless you address both of these challenges, unless you see the way they are intertwined, your life will be as unbalanced as that of someone climbing onto a bicycle with a missing wheel. This book thus seeks to create something new: to merge the separate genres that isolate your bank statement from your inner life, your spiritual quest from your material needs, your money from your life's meaning.

My Journey

Many years ago I read Bob Buford's classic *Halftime*, which describes the interval when we retreat to the locker room to assess the first half of our lives and plan for the second. While I found it interesting and thought-provoking, it didn't resonate with me at the time. Fast-forward to 2012. My fiftieth birthday was right around the corner, and something made me pick up the book again. This time the message shook me to my core. I had hit my own personal "halftime," and the implications were huge.

To use my earlier metaphor, I was like someone who had walked off the stage to tremendous applause after the first act of a Shakespearean play. I was full of pride and a sense of accomplishment until I realized the drama had only just begun—the bulk of the action and excitement still lay ahead of me. Yet I'd only prepared for the opening scene. I couldn't just walk back out and recite the same lines over again. But the curtain was going up. What was I to do? I was a one-act performer in a five-act play.

Of course, I'm not an athlete at halftime or a performer between acts. I'm a financial advisor. All the same, I had a nagging sense that something was missing from the way I worked with my clients. My technical qualifications were first-rate. I had graduated from the University of Georgia, held three respected professional designations,[4] and was pursuing a master's degree in financial planning. Having worked for a large company, I'd developed the skills and confidence to establish my own successful business in 2003: I was the founder, president, and chief investment officer in TandemGrowth Financial Advisors. I was an expert in helping clients manage risk, develop tax and legacy plans, create a lifelong income stream, and many other matters. By 2005 I could see that my business was going to thrive.

So why wasn't I satisfied?

My first epiphany came that same year when I went to a conference in San Francisco. I arrived a day early, so I went to the Japanese Tea Garden in Golden Gate Park and spent several hours reflecting on questions that are all too easy to ignore in the course of a hectic

---

4   Certified Financial Planner™, Charter Financial Consultant, and Certified Funds Specialist.

workweek: Why does my firm exist? What is my role? Was I doing all I could to serve the most profound needs of my clients?

Before I left the park, I'd started answering these questions. I realized that I wanted to be more than a traditional financial advisor, that my calling was deeper than that. I realized that I'd been given great opportunities to help people, but I'd focused exclusively on material matters—as if money were an end in itself rather than the means to an end. Like other firms, we were doing great work helping people get the trappings of success—we were enabling them to retire, educate their children, buy second homes, and avoid money worries—but I realized we should be doing much more than that.

By the time I returned home, I decided we were going to change the way TandemGrowth served clients. Our mission would now be to help people align their actions and resources with what mattered most in their lives. Now this didn't mean we would compromise one iota on the quality of our financial advice. But I wanted to broaden my job description. I wanted to be a better steward of my God-given talents and expertise.

I realized that to be fulfilled in the second act of my life, I needed to do more than help rich people get richer and successful people add to their roster of achievements. I needed to help them live happier lives. In essence the discovery of my own deeper purpose—helping mid- to late-career business professionals create the freedom to pursue their own calling—coincided with the insight that what many of my clients lacked, often without realizing it, was precisely what I had begun to discover: a sense of their own true mission. And without that, no amount of wealth could allay their discomfort and bring them happiness.

The Path Forward

Every year my wife meticulously decorates our Christmas tree, turning it into a work of art. Of course, she can't perform her magic until the tree has been set up and she's had time to study its conformation. Only then can she decide what ornament best goes where, how the tinsel can be strategically arranged to complement the tree's unique features. Similarly, when the holidays are over, she meticulously wraps and boxes up our more costly decorations so that they survive until the next Christmas. Not until that point am I called in to do my disassembly work and drag the tree out to the curb. On both sides of the process, first things must come first.

That's the principle on which I've structured this book. In part 1, we'll explore foundational issues, such as enjoying the journey of your life rather than struggling toward some imaginary finish line after which you'll (supposedly) be showered in happiness. Just as my wife needs to study the tree before she starts decorating it, so we all need to clarify what motivates us, what gets us up in the morning, what purpose our money will serve before we can sensibly work out a financial plan. Too often, however, people in my industry skip this step—with dire consequences for their clients. Midas made a quick decision about how to maximize his wealth. Turning all he touched to gold sounded better in the abstract than it did when he kissed his children and sat down to eat. Yet somehow the message of that simple allegory often gets lost when we consider our own lives.

To avoid that fate, we'll explore how wealth and joy can grow together. I'll talk about the hero's journey of discovery, what you can expect on the road, and the importance of having a guide who has made a similar quest and knows the terrain. I'll relate episodes of my own ongoing quest as we travel together toward more purpose-filled lives. We'll explore the importance of listening to both the head and the heart, the intuitive and creative right brain and the logical left. Most importantly we'll distinguish the deeper needs of the spirit from the superficial demands of the ego, the false self from the true.

Part 2 will provide practical methods for conducting your own inner excavation that will help you to discover your unique strengths and passions, to clarify a vision of what gives *your* life meaning—as distinct from a generic sense of what other people consider impressive or important. In chapter 8, we'll also examine how to build the capacity to turn that vision into reality, how to create the time, resources, and energy to pursue the goals that make you come alive. Along the way we'll explore a wide range of topics—from uncovering your true calling to what I call contemplative "desert days," from an exploration of values to building an ideal week—that can help enrich and sustain your quest.

Having clarified your core beliefs and capacities, having placed first things first, we'll move to part 3: a wealth management toolbox. Here I'll draw on my thirty-six years of experience as a financial advisor to take a holistic approach to your second act. We'll explore goal-focused planning, retirement income planning, tax planning, risk management, and estate planning.

Figure 1.1 What is included in a holistic wealth management plan?

I'll devote a separate chapter to evidence-based investing so you don't make the all-too-common mistake of treating your hard-earned savings like a stack of chips in a Las Vegas casino. I'll conclude with an explanation about why I'm a rational optimist, how psychological and biological factors can thwart wise investment decisions, and why doing less is often better than doing more in the world of investing. In essence part 3 will provide the financial information to help you pursue the larger purposes we've identified in part 1 and part 2.

"Midway through life's journey, I found I had lost my way"[5]—thus begins perhaps the greatest poem ever written, Dante Alighieri's *Divine Comedy*, composed in 1320. With the help of his guide, Virgil, the hero, Dante, reorients himself and emerges from the depths of despair, climbs the slopes of purgatory, and ascends to the gates of heaven and a blissful union with God.

The poem generates much of its power because it describes a universal, archetypal experience: we all confront a sense of confusion when we complete the opening act of our lives. Midway through our journeys, we often lose our way. Whether we regain a sense of clarity and purpose depends on how we respond to that loss. In the pages that follow, we'll work together to emerge from the darkness and reenter the light.

Let's get started.

---

5   Dante Alighieri, *The Divine Comedy*, translated by Allen Mandelbaum (New York: Bantam Books, 1982).

CHAPTER 2

Financial Peace and Meaning in Tandem

Riches and abundance come hypocritically clad in sheep's clothing, pretending to be security against anxieties, and they become then the object of anxiety. They secure a man against anxieties just about as well as the wolf that is put to tending the sheep.

—SØREN KIERKEGAARD [6]

Quality Time

One Sunday afternoon, when I was a young parent, I'd set aside time to do some quiet reading. Instead, I found myself increasingly annoyed by the repeated interruptions of my children. Every few minutes they'd charge into the room with a distracting question or comment that broke my concentration: "Hey, Dad, can we have some

---

6   Søren Kierkegaard, *The Quotable Kierkegaard* (Princeton, New Jersey: Princeton University Press, 2013).

ice cream? Hey, Dad, why is the sky blue? Hey, Dad, why don't your socks match? Hey, Dad, will you play catch with us?"

No parent will be surprised by this news: kids are full of energy and mischief. They want and deserve our attention. Nonetheless, after fifteen minutes of rereading the same two sentences, my patience was running out. I sighed and looked out the window. Only then did the irony hit me: my kids' needs were distracting me from reading a book about how to be a good father. More specifically, the chapter I was earnestly trying to parse was about spending "quality time" with my family. Smiling at myself, I put down the book, fixed them some ice cream, checked my socks (they matched!), and went outside to play catch—hoping I could remember why the sky was blue.

As we start our money and meaning journey together, I want you to avoid the mistake I just described. This isn't a book to be consumed in one or two sittings. In fact, many times the best strategy will be to close the text, go outside, relax, and contemplate how the ideas I've introduced relate to the particulars of your life. I'll still be here when you come back! Strange as it may sound, my goal is not that of the typical author: I'm not trying to compose something you find "impossible to put down."

Quite the opposite.

Of course, I want to hold your attention and provide you with useful information, but I'm equally concerned with what you do in the intervals between reading. Again and again I'm going to point you back to your own experience. In trying to align your finances with your higher calling, I'll be appealing to both your head and your heart, your creative and intuitive right brain, and your orderly and rational left brain. I'll count myself successful if you spend more time reflecting on and applying the concepts I raise than you do poring over the text.

As Saint Irenaeus of Lyons wrote in the second century, "The glory of God is man fully alive."[7] Was I fully alive when *reading* about being a good parent prevented me from *responding* to the needs of my children? Of course not. I was locked in my head and cut off from my heart. Pursuing the ideal, I had lost track of the real.

I eventually finished the book. I learned a lot, and I did in fact become a better father (at least I hope so). But the most important lesson was the one my children taught me: reading was a *preparation* for living, not a *substitute* for it. Meeting a daily quota of pages read can be counterproductive if you use it as an excuse to avoid the harder and more important challenge: discovering your true self, aligning your means with your meaning, and becoming "fully alive."

A Logo for a Full Life

The image in my firm's logo will help me convey a balanced approach, particularly if you understand how its symbolic import has evolved over time. Originally I chose the drawing of two trees growing side by side to represent the symbiotic relationship between my company and our clients: we would grow together financially in a mutually beneficial manner. The broadening and symmetrical canopy of leaves demonstrated the fulfillment of a common purpose.

That meaning still holds true today. But I now see that what originally appealed to me in the logo was an aspiration toward something deeper and richer than I could fully appreciate at the time. I'm not comparing myself with Jefferson, Adams, Hamilton, Washington, and the other founders of our nation, but just as the Declaration of Independence and the US Constitution expressed ideals of liberty beyond

---

7   Irenaeus of Lyons, *Against Heresies*, Book 4, Chapter 34, Section 7 (Pickerington, Ohio: Beloved Press, 2014). The line is sometimes translated as "For the glory of God is the living man, and the life of man is the vision of God."

what the framers might have consciously understood, my logo was in some ways wiser than the ambitious financial advisor who selected it.

Figure 2.1 A logo for a full life.

Though I've always cultivated trusting relationships with my clients, though I've always considered their long-term interests, TandemGrowth's original mission was much like that of many other businesses in my field: our focus was largely on money rather than meaning. Following the epiphany I described in the introduction, however, I saw that the logo had always foreshadowed—and perhaps even helped me recognize—my emerging desire to develop a holistic approach to my work. Today those side-by-side trees also represent the twin components of a happy life: identifying our larger purpose and achieving the financial means necessary to fulfill that purpose. Pursuing either at the expense of the other is a recipe for frustration and suffering.

An Epidemic of Affluenza

Our modern age has given birth to a new word that describes an increasingly common affliction, one that occurs when our compulsive pursuit of money and material objects becomes detached from any real sense of what gives our lives meaning. Combining the wealth of *affluence* with the disease of *influenza*, the term *affluenza* "describes a condition of extreme materialism and consumerism associated with the pursuit of wealth and success and resulting in a life of chronic dissatisfaction, debt, overwork, stress, and impaired relationships."[8]

In terms of the balanced life symbolized in our logo, affluenza occurs when the tree of wealth begins to grow all out of proportion to the tree of meaning, blocking out the sun and destroying any sense of harmony. If our designer had presented us with an image of one towering and healthy tree beside a withering and leafless one, even my untrained sense of aesthetics would have recoiled. Sadly, however, many of us who would reject that disturbing visual seem unable to recognize the way it often mirrors our lopsided lives.

My purpose here is simply to describe the disease. In the chapters that follow, I'll provide a process to identify and overcome it in your own life. Why should you trust me? Because my expertise as a diagnostician has been hard won. And I'm not referring to library research or merely observing the symptoms in my clients. Painful as it is to admit, I'm a recovering affluenza sufferer myself.

When I was younger and first achieving some success, I decided scuba diving would make me happy. I spent thousands of dollars on fancy equipment. I bought a state-of-the-art camera, deep-sea watches, a dive computer, and on and on. Each purchase promised

---

8   Merriam-Webster's Online Dictionary (https://www.merriam-webster.com/dictionary/affluenza).

to make the experience more enjoyable. That was what the advertisers told me. Surely they wouldn't lie! So I just kept piling up stuff as if I were about to join Jacques Cousteau's team on the *Calypso*.

Where is all that gear now? Piled in the garage like a monument to my acquisitiveness. I enjoyed the hobby for a season or two, but ultimately it just wasn't for me. For oceanographers, scuba diving may be intimately connected with their higher calling. For me, it was primarily a distraction.

Did that insight cure me of my affluenza? No. Like the self-destructive smoker who wants a cigarette even while he is smoking one (should he put two in his mouth?), my craving was boundless, misdirected, and impossible to satisfy. Blind to this futility, oblivious of my higher purpose, I simply replaced one compulsion with another. I was on a quest for more, more, more—more clients, a more prestigious business award, a more impressive credential, a larger company, a bigger house, a better car, more admiration from my peers. Fulfillment was always waiting for me over the next horizon—and then the one after that.

I was on the "hedonic treadmill,"[9] a phrase coined by behavioral psychologists Philip Brickman and Donald T. Campbell to describe the futility—like running in place—of blindly and energetically struggling to find happiness in possessions and achievements that were cut off from my larger purpose. An overwhelming body of research shows that just as increasing your pace on a treadmill doesn't change your position in space, so the accumulation of trophies and treasure—beyond what's required to meet our basic needs—doesn't budge the needle on our fulfillment gauge. Unless we find our God-inspired purpose, however, most of us simply lack any other strategy for fulfill-

---

9   Philip Brickman and Donald T. Campbell, *Hedonic Relativism and Planning the Good Society* (New York: Academic Press, 1971).

ment, so we simply repeat the same process in accordance with the oft-cited definition of insanity: doing the same thing over and over and expecting a different result.

I want to emphasize that as a financial advisor, I'm not arguing that you join the Jesuit priests by taking an oath of poverty or that you renounce all your worldly possessions, move to a commune, and sing kumbaya around the campfire each night. I'm in the business of helping people increase their wealth, and my company has a proven record of doing just that. Being able to provide the best life for your family is a noble and important accomplishment. And I'm no Puritan: there's nothing wrong with having fun—or taking up scuba diving. My point is that unless you are committed to something higher than the demands of your ego or the desire to distract yourself from the monotony of a directionless life, no amount of money is going to put your emotional life in the black. Like someone with a brain tumor that manifests itself as numbness in your hands, you'll waste a lot of time speaking with orthopedic surgeons and massage therapists when what you really need is a neurologist. Only when you recognize that

When we let possessions (i.e., "things") drive our lives, we're like a dismounted rider who harnesses the saddle to his own back.

mistake can you stop treating the symptoms and start focusing on the cause. Only then can you recover from affluenza and find peace.

The transcendental philosopher and poet Ralph Waldo Emerson beautifully expressed the absurdity of allowing our lives to fall out of sync with our own higher calling. When we let possessions (i.e., "things") drive our lives, we're like a dismounted rider who harnesses the saddle to his own back; in such a world, Emerson says everything is backward:

The horseman serves the horse.
The merchant serves the purse.
Web to weave, and corn to grind,
Things are in the saddle,
And ride mankind.[10]

Enough Is Enough

Unfortunately, I often meet with people who seem unaware that they are carrying their horses, that they are serving their money rather than allowing it to serve them. It's sad. I think about all the work they've done to get to this point in their lives. They've planned for their future, saved their money, and made sacrifices. They're entitled to financial peace, but they don't experience it. Rather than discovering and pursuing their Act 2 calling, they remain stuck in Act 1. As a result, they are chronically anxious. They spend much of their time watching the business news. They worry—"Have I made enough money? Have I invested it in the right places?" They're focused on markets and catastrophes and all the things that can go wrong. Or like my client who spends part of every year miserable about what a hurricane might do to his second home in Florida, they worry about controlling a future over which they have no control.

Their tree of wealth may be thriving, but they can't recognize that because their tree of meaning is stunted. Absent a higher purpose on which to focus their energies, they continue to fight a war they've already won. Their subsequent "triumphs" thus feel hollow, redundant, and even self-destructive—like those of the Greek general Pyrrhus,

---

10 Ralph Waldo Emerson, "Ode to William H. Channing," in *Collected Poems and Translations* (New York: Library of America, 1994).

who defeated a Roman legion in 279 BCE, scanned the battlefield, assessed the costs of his success in the corpses of his soldiers, and wryly remarked, "A few more victories like this and we are done for."[11]

Kurt Vonnegut wrote a short poem whose title is the name of a fellow writer: "Joe Heller."[12] The piece points toward a respite from such interminable struggles. At a party thrown by a billionaire, Vonnegut attempts to goad Heller about the relative paltriness of his financial achievements compared with their wealthy host. Heller responds:

> And Joe said, "I've got something he can never have."
> And I said, "What on earth could that be, Joe?"
> And Joe said, "The knowledge that I've got enough."

Such knowledge most often comes when you've met two preconditions: identifying and embarking on your Act 2 mission and establishing the financial peace of mind that allows you to stop struggling with needless worries and start reveling in your newfound freedom.

Of course, we all have individual answers to the question, "How much is enough?" If you have elderly parents to support or children or grandchildren to put through college, that figure may be higher than for those without such commitments. The same may be true if you have set high philanthropic goals such as supporting a church or a charity. Do you want to donate your time at a local foodbank or establish a new cancer research center that bears your name? Do you prefer to stay at home, or do you value unique travel experiences with your family—visiting the Egyptian pyramids, the Vatican in Rome,

---

11   Plutarch, *Plutarch's Lives: Complete and Unabridged* (New York: Random House, 1975).

12   Kurt Vonnegut, "Joe Heller," *The New Yorker*, May 16, 2005.

Victoria Falls in Zambia, or Machu Picchu in Peru? If you live in San Francisco, you'll face a higher cost of living than someone in rural Georgia. You'll want to discuss these and myriad other variables with a financial advisor.

But your life's meaning will always shape the means you require to achieve it. Ignoring that connection is like trying to pack your suitcase for an unknown destination. Are you heading to the Swiss Alps or the beaches of Maui? Are you meeting with the yachting set in Monaco or visiting the Buddhist monks in Tibet for a silent retreat? You can't prepare your suitcase or your Act 2 life unless you can answer some fundamental questions. By the time you finish this book, you'll be off to a great start.

In the next chapter, we'll look more closely at something I wish I had learned much earlier in life: how to live in the present moment, how to distinguish our true self from our false self, how to see beneath the carefully contrived mask most of us present to the world when we confuse the fleeting demands of our egos with the timeless messages of our souls.

CHAPTER 3

Replace "Fake It Till You Make It" with the "Immortal Diamond"

Those who have not found true wealth, which is the radiant joy of Being and the deep, unshakable peace that comes with it, are beggars, even if they have great material wealth.
—ECKHART TOLLE[13]

An April Fool

Although I couldn't fully appreciate the irony at the time, I started my career as a financial advisor on April Fools' Day 1986. Back then, the industry coached us to "fake it till you make it." In other words, we should put on an act, play a fictitious role, show the world a false

---

13   Eckhart Tolle, *The Power of Now: A Guide to Spiritual Enlightenment* (Novato, California: New World Library, 2004).

face. We should ignore who we actually were in the present moment for the sake of who we intended to become in the future.

So that was exactly what I did. I had just turned twenty-three, but I brazenly leased a new Volvo. After all, what says super-sophisticated, mature "finance guy" like a Volvo? That worn-out Oldsmobile Cutlass my father bought for me before I started college simply wasn't an adequate chariot for someone advising more experienced clients twice my age. I'm lucky there were no Rolls-Royce dealers in town.

Nor was my foolishness restricted to car purchases. As a would-be master of the financial universe, someone determined to impress prospective clients, I certainly wasn't going to show up at my office in some pedestrian, off-the-rack suit. Since my manager and mentor wore custom-made clothes, surely I should wear them as well. Everyone knows that "clothes make the man," right? At work, I used complicated and unhelpful financial jargon so that my older clients would think I was a prodigy, a wunderkind. I joined Atlanta's posh Ravinia Club so I could take those same clients out to lavish lunches and dinners that I'd never have eaten on my own.

Although I managed to build a reasonably successful practice for the first part of my career, I was basically just doing what the world told me I needed to do to "be successful." I was an empty suit, a papier-mâché guy, what T. S. Eliot calls one of the "hollow men." I was an excellent chameleon, but was a reptilian life strategy really going to fulfill my deeper needs? In my desire to impress others, was I even acknowledging those needs?

Of course, there's nothing wrong with nice cars, fine clothes, expensive restaurants, and so on. I still enjoy them. I'm no Puritan recommending you don a hair shirt and renounce all worldly pleasures. What I am suggesting, however, is that a life founded exclusively on fakery, ephemera, and the trappings of success as defined by others will eventually backfire and leave you miserable. No Puritan life of denial is less joyful than that. I know from experience, however, that shifting into autopilot to meet day-to-day business challenges can become a kind of spiritual hibernation from which some of us never awaken. To greater or lesser degrees, many of the mid- to late-career executives I meet have been faking it much of their lives too, ignoring their moment-by-moment experiences in pursuit of a constantly receding future in which they will start enjoying themselves. Once you start playing a role, it can be hard to quit.

In this chapter, we'll contrast the inevitable emptiness that comes from faking it with the rewards of discovering what the poet Gerard Manley Hopkins calls "the immortal diamond" that we all have within us every second of our lives but that, tragically, we often fail to see. Eckhart Tolle sketches the dimensions of that tragedy when he says that those who fail to discover this diamond end up "looking outside for scraps of pleasure or fulfillment, for validation, security, or love, while they have a treasure within that not only includes all of those things, but is infinitely greater than anything the world could offer."

Be Authentic

If I could go back and speak to my younger self, I'd point out the futility and self-destructiveness of the fake-it strategy. At the most basic level, I'd explain that I hadn't been fooling anyone. Were my experienced clients—all of whom knew I was a year out of college—really fooled by my car, my suit, my financial jargon, and my club memberships? Did they see the twenty-three-year-old me as a wizened and wily veteran of the money management wars? Of course not—no more than my childhood neighbors were fooled by the pirate costume I'd worn on Halloween. I have no doubt that many of the people I worked with in those early years had to suppress a smile at my pre-posterous youthful pretentions.

My clients worked with me *in spite of* my false uniform, not *because of* it. What interested them were precisely the authentic qualities I was at pains to hide: my youthful energy and enthusiasm, my willingness to work long hours on their behalf, my eagerness to make up for my lack of experience with on-the-job study and diligence. They worked with me for who I was—an idealistic kid—not for the person I was pretending to be. The only person taken in by my performance was me.

On a deeper level, I'd tell my youthful self what I tell all my employees, regardless of age: be who God created you to be. Tell the unvarnished truth. If you don't know something, say so. Be authentic. You're already good enough. Your deeper purpose has always been present within you. People will respond to that, provided you've taken the time and done the soul-searching necessary to discover it yourself. Devote your energy to that project rather than wasting time dressing up in someone else's clothes. You'll spare yourself a lot of stress and be a better steward of your own resources and of those with whom you associate. A quote often falsely attributed to Oscar Wilde is applicable here: "Be yourself; everyone else is already taken."[14] What Wilde actually said is even more compelling: "It is tragic how few people ever 'possess their souls' before they die."[15] The tragedy is especially keen because we all can avoid that fate by simply being authentic, by dropping our fake-it strategies and looking inward.

---

[14] The source of the quote is unknown—though the Trappist monk Thomas Merton said something similar: "For me sanctity consists in being myself and for you sanctity consists in being yourself and ... your sanctity will never be mine, and mine will never be yours." Thomas Merton, *The New Seeds of Contemplation* (New York: New Directions Publishing, 1949).

[15] Oscar Wilde, *The Complete Letters of Oscar Wide* (New York: Henry Holt and Company, 2000).

Unfortunately, I suspect my youthful self would have nodded politely but never fully absorbed this advice. Caught up in the demands of my ego and spurred on by social incentives, I'd likely have pretended to listen while all the time planning how I would continue down what I "knew" to be the correct path as soon as this old fellow stopped jawing in my ear. No doubt there are young spiritual adepts capable of grasping these insights, but I was not one of them.

Nor are many of the mid- to late-career people I encounter. Indeed, a large number of them—successful though they be on many metrics—often feel inauthentic and unfulfilled. They've impressed the world without managing to satisfy themselves. They've met the social markers of success, but they aren't feeling the sense of achievement and joy they anticipated. Having failed to discover what they've never been encouraged to find—their higher purpose—at some deep level, they feel as if they are still faking it. And at some deep level, they are correct.

That's because most of us have to "make it" before we begin to question the value of what we've made. Only in midcareer—fueled by our frustration—do we see beyond generic, socially approved ideals and begin the quest for the larger individual purpose holocaust survivor and psychotherapist Viktor Frankl identified in the title of his most famous work: *Man's Search for Meaning*. Once we discover the meaning specific to ourselves (the focus of part 2 of this book), our lives can flourish under any circumstances—even within the barbed wire confines of a Nazi concentration camp. But until we do so, no country club membership, scuba diving gear, improved golf score, public acclaim, or expensive vacation will enable us to escape what Frankl calls the "Sunday neurosis, that kind of depression which afflicts people who become aware of the lack of content in their lives when the rush of the busy week is over and the void within themselves becomes manifest."[16]

Don't misunderstand me: I don't think the ego or the false self is evil. They are absolutely necessary, especially in Act 1. They just aren't who you really are. The antidote to Frankl's "neurosis" is to recognize that our lives are unbalanced. We've spent so much time looking outward and into the future for our cues and affirmations that we've failed to cultivate—or even notice—our inner resources. The good news is that the guiding light of the immortal diamond we all possess does not have an expiration date. This diamond has been called many names: our soul, our true self, the holy spirit within, or our divine nature. Whatever name we use, the crucial point is this: Nothing we do—or fail to do—can extinguish that light. We didn't build the immortal diamond. We don't have to earn it. All we have to do is slow down and attend to it.

Some of us discover the immortal diamond, our true self, only after we've grown discontent with the flimsy, breakable baubles and cheap glass beads of conventional success. By simply attending to our own authentic impulses, our lives become more joyful.

Presence Is Our Essence

Our attention is a form of reverence. Simone Weil likens it to prayer.[17] We honor ourselves when we attend to our authentic needs as they arise. We honor others by being fully attentive to them, undistracted by our cell phones, our text messages, our daydreams, the conversations we had yesterday, and our plans for tomorrow. We learn from

---

16   Viktor E. Frankl, *Man's Search for Meaning* (Boston, Massachusetts: Beacon Press, 1949).

17   Simone Weil, *Gravity and Grace* (Oxfordshire, England: Routledge and CRC Press, 2002).

our past, we motivate ourselves by thoughts of the future, but we live our lives in the present, the now. That's the only place we can ever discover our essence, our immortal diamond. That's the only place our lives will ever be available to us.

When we show a false self to the world, we squander the potential joys available in each moment of our journey for an idealized notion of some future perfection. We dismiss, ignore, and foolishly sacrifice the present moment as something to be endured for the sake of a distant payoff. Moreover, that far-off oasis of content is usually impoverished by our narrow projections of what constitutes an ideal life. Having set our sights on a false paradise, we can all too easily blind ourselves to more immediate and gratifying sources of happiness. It's easy to miss what we've determined—consciously or unconsciously—isn't worth seeing.

When we show a false self to the world, we squander the potential joys available in each moment of our journey for an idealized notion of some future perfection.

This is my Achilles' heel, and I invite you to question whether it may be yours as well. You might take a moment right now and notice if you're really focused on this sentence or if you're being pulled back obsessively—like a dog chasing its tail—into some past experience you can't change and from which you've already extracted all there is to learn. Or perhaps you're being pulled forward, imagining how you'll apply the insights of the next chapter, which you haven't yet read, to money and meaning challenges that may never arise. If something demands your immediate attention, by all means put down the book and attend to it. But give that issue your full attention rather than once again distracting yourself, perhaps by being annoyed that you've stopped reading a book you've just acknowledged you are too distracted to follow. A life in which you spend every moment preoccupied with some other moment will always produce a kind of hell on earth.

It's essential to have goals, but once we've set them, we need to return to the *now* and fully inhabit the ongoing series of present moments that lead to that goal. To do otherwise is to forfeit our actual lives for the airy phantoms of future lives over which we have little control. Even though I know this, I often catch myself sleepwalking through the day, becoming so outcome-focused and obsessed by my goals that I barely notice what's going on around me. Rather than enjoying the process of working toward my objectives, I can all too easily turn the goal into a fetish, slipping away into unproductive and unhappy ruminations about the past or empty projections—both of horrible disasters and transcendent glories—about the future. To paraphrase T. S. Eliot, I'm having experiences but missing their meaning.

Consider the example of the wealthy and imminently successful Charles E. Merrill, the cofounder of the investing firm Merrill Lynch. According to his son, the writer James Merrill, Charles was chronically restless and dissatisfied in spite of his many accomplishments. Without being fully able to enjoy his achievements, his friendships, and his multiple marriages, Charles died of a heart attack while "*in his prime* at three score ten." In a piece called "The Broken Home," James writes, "Time was money in those days ... but money was not time."[18] Recognizing the intransitive relationship between time and money is a necessary condition for true financial peace. And that peace can only ever occur in the *now*.

---

18   James Merrill, *Collected Poems* (New York: Knopf, 2001).

Discovering My Why: A Tale of Two Vacations

Some of you may recall Clark Griswold, the main character in *National Lampoon's Vacation*, a satirical film released in 1983. Clark plans the "perfect" vacation. He maps out precisely where and when his family will stop at every moment of their road trip from Chicago to a famous Southern California amusement park, "Wally World," modeled after Disneyland.

The Griswolds spend precisely two minutes at the Grand Canyon. The family rushes out of the car, stares at this natural wonder for the predetermined interval, absorbs the appropriate dose of splendor, crosses the site off their list, and races back to the car as if guided by a stopwatch and a "fun's over" buzzer. Then it's on to Old Faithful so they can efficiently arrive at the precise moment it erupts. The madness continues in this vein until they reach the amusement park, which is closed.

Satire that's easy to spot on the screen often proves difficult to spot in our lives. I hate to admit it, but almost twenty years after I laughed at the movie, I became Clark Griswold. In 2001 I planned the perfect Disney World vacation. At the time my children were two and four, and my parents had rented a place nearby. I had every day planned. I had the maps. I had the schedules. I knew when we could get early admission to certain parts of the park, when we were going to take the kids home for naps, and how long those naps should last so we could get back to the park for the nightly fireworks.

I remember being in the line for the Haunted Mansion and anxiously thinking, "Oh no. There's a really long line. We're going to be late for the 2:12 show at the Country Bear Jamboree." Everything was synchronized: I treated the trip as if I were a general leading his troops into a battle rather than a father trying to enjoy a trip with his family.

The German philosopher Friedrich Nietzsche might have clarified my problem if I'd recalled his aphorism, "He who has a *why* to live can bear almost any *how*."[19] I'd answered the *what* and *how* questions about my trip, but I'd completely lost track of the more fundamental *why* question. My *what* goal was to have a great vacation, my *how* goal was spelled out in my ruthless itinerary, but what was my *why*? I'd completely lost sight of that.

In retrospect the obvious answer is *I wanted to get closer to my children, my wife, and my parents*. But my obsession with having the perfect trip all but guaranteed that this wouldn't happen, that in fact the trip would become a Clark Griswold fiasco. How could it not? I simply wasn't present with the people I loved. I wasn't sharing the moments we had together. Trapped in my outcome-focused mind, I was cut off from my heart. So what if we didn't get a perfect photo of Mickey Mouse? The real tragedy was that, with the best of intentions, I was missing an opportunity to connect with my family. My kids were full of whimsy, and I was looking miserably at my watch, trying to make sure we didn't miss out on any fun.

I'm sad to say that many successful executives begin their Act 2 lives in this same grim posture. Like me on the Disney trip, they're not enjoying the now. They're stressed out or gritting their teeth to achieve what the retirement brochures advertise as happiness. And that's just another form of faking it. That's just another kind of Volvo. They're still not connecting with their immortal diamond. As the Franciscan priest Richard Rohr says, once they do, they'll understand that "[t]he True Self does not cling or grasp. It has already achieved its purpose by being more than by any specific doing of this or that. Finally, we have become a human *being* instead of a human *doing*."[20]

---

19   Fredrich Nietzsche, *The Twilight of the Idols* (New York: Penguin Classics, 1990).

20   Richard Rohr, Center for Action and Contemplation, https://cac.org/lesson-three-your-life-is-hidden-with-christ-2020-04-08/.

It took me some time, but I'm happy to report that even Clark Griswold can change. In 2019 my wife and I planned our dream trip to Italy. This time, instead of preparing for a Bataan Death March, I enjoyed the preparation process. I did everything on my own. I didn't use an agent. I found resources and an excellent guide. I did everything in the spirit of adventure. We went from Venice to the Amalfi Coast, so we covered a lot of territory. But I was totally present. My son, Nick, went with us, and I just enjoyed being with him and my wife. And if we were having fun in one place, we reveled in the moment. We canceled a couple of things to prolong those moments. We were spontaneous. We banished Clark Griswold. We found our *why*. Helping you to do the same is one of the aims of this book.

In the next chapter, we'll look more closely at how all our lives follow the archetype of "the hero's journey" and at how to set forth on that journey so that our Act 2 lives bring us the true richness we crave and deserve.

CHAPTER 4

The Hero's Journey

The journey of the hero is about the courage to seek the depths; the image of creative rebirth; the eternal cycle of change within us ... "always the one, shape-shifting yet marvelously constant story that we find."

—JOSEPH CAMPBELL[21]

You Are the Hero

At all times, in all places, cultures have produced stories that captivate audiences, not only in their own era but also across the ages. From parables in the religious scriptures of every faith to the *Odyssey*, from the plays of Shakespeare to the novels of Charles Dickens and the melodramatic operas of Mozart, from movies such as *The Wizard of Oz*, *The Lord of the Rings*, *Star Wars*, and *Band of Brothers* to your favorite detective series on Netflix—all these narratives share a basic architecture or archetype, what anthropologists refer to as a "monomyth"

---

21   Joseph Campbell, *The Hero with a Thousand Faces* (Novato, California: New World Library, 2008).

and Joseph Campbell calls "the hero's journey." To simplify a bit, we can say that the central character begins in an ordinary world (e.g., Dorothy in Kansas), is called forth on an adventure, briefly resists that call, finds a trustworthy guide, struggles to discover something of great importance, and returns home—transformed by the journey.

Why do we find this pattern so engaging? Because, consciously or not, it reenacts the struggle of our own lives, however mundane they may feel. We may not be Achilles on the battlefield at Troy, but his story resonates with us because we all face crises and trials, endure periods of frustration, question our core beliefs, seek help from a wise advisor, and, if we are to thrive, emerge from this internal or external journey with hard-won insights about who we are and how we should live.

In this chapter I'm going to adapt the journey paradigm established by Campbell and others to the spiritual and psychological lives of those in the mid to late stages of their careers. In chapter 5 I'll shift my focus from the *meaning* questions to the equally important challenges related to *money*. You, dear reader, are the hero of both of these chapters. Drawing on my own ongoing struggles with the same trials you're facing and on my decades of experience helping others align their means with their life's meaning, I'm offering this book as a guide. Together we'll enter the dark and unfamiliar forest that divides our Act 1 lives from the vast possibilities that await us in the subsequent acts.

> We shall not cease from exploration
> And the end of all our exploring
> Will be to arrive where we started
> And know the place for the first time.[22]

---

22   T. S. Eliot, *Four Quartets* (Mariner Books, 1968).

My Hero's Background

Since you are my hero and I am your guide, let's begin by discussing the common threads in our backstories. When we were young, we struggled to understand and define *who* we were, *what* talents and interests we had, *how* we could cultivate and apply those talents, *where* we would focus our energies, and *when* we had gained sufficient expertise to begin making our way in the world.

This is a period of discovery—both painful and exhilarating. Maybe we wanted to be professional athletes or theoretical physicists, but our mediocre performance on the playground or the merciful C- the kindly math teacher bestowed on us in calculus class suggest we weren't cut out to be the next Michael Jordan or Albert Einstein. On the other hand, we may discover an unexpected gift for leadership and find that we enjoy the challenges of bringing out the best in others much more than we do missing shamefully easy layups in a high school gym or trying to understand the abstract relationship between time and motion or whatever it is that happens inside black holes.

So we head off to college, take the appropriate battery of courses necessary to become adept in the field we've chosen, graduate, and join the workforce. Now we begin a period of rapid ascent: our paychecks grow, we earn promotions and praise, we accumulate various awards, and perhaps we start our own successful businesses. We buy houses and cars. We develop new hobbies and join country clubs. In Campbell's terms, we've left the ordinary world of childhood, received a call to self-defining action, made some missteps, found professors and mentors to serve as guides, met a series of challenges, and emerged into adulthood, transformed by what we've experienced. We began as caterpillars and have metamorphosed into beautiful monarch butterflies free to fly from flower to flower.

End of story?

Nothing to do now except live, as the fairy tales say, "happily ever after"?

Hardly.

As I clarified in the previous chapter, most of us enter this phase of life still burdened by a number of fake-it strategies and self-delusions, which may take us years to recognize given the apparent "perfection" of our careers and the affirmation of our colleagues and friends. In many ruinous cases, we carry those delusions to our graves. Nonetheless, we've successfully started the first stage of our journey.

Only now does the essential quest of our adult lives begin to emerge, often in the restlessness and smoldering discontent we discussed earlier. Like Odysseus lost in the momentarily satisfying but ultimately self-destructive pleasures on the island of the narcotic lotus-eaters, we are still far from home. Many of us are neglecting our God-inspired purpose. We're moving through the scenes of Act 1, but the play is just beginning.

S Curves versus Artificial Finish Lines

The graphic below depicts the stages crucial to completing the hero's journey and the potential pitfalls that often block that completion. As we've discussed, Act 1 begins with a period of learning and capability building, followed by a rapid ascent. All seems to be going well until the vast majority of us reach a crisis at point *A*. The precise nature of this crisis can vary widely—an illness, a divorce, the death of a loved one, a sense of stagnation, or inauthenticity—anything that forces us to question the status quo most of us have upheld in Act 1. What happens at this crossroad will in large part determine the hero's fate.

ACT 1 AND DONE

Those who fail to discover—or refuse to accept—their God-inspired purpose will grit their teeth and persist in their original strategy, hoping against hope that what has failed them in the past will somehow reward them in the future. Though their material fortunes may continue to rise for a time, their lives become increasingly hollow and devoid of meaning. Like the tales of disoriented explorers searching the same seas for the fictitious island of Atlantis, their stories generally follow a predictable downward trajectory to point B: unhappy retirement, midlife crises, burnout, despair, and loss of identity.[23]

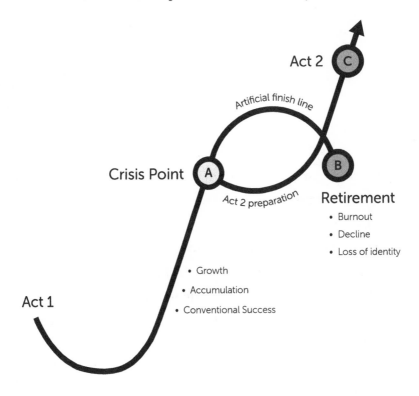

Figure 4.1 The hero's journey.

---

23   I am indebted to the Halftime Institute for the graph's structure, which I have modified to suit my own terminology and themes.

Mitch Anthony refers to arc AB as the "artificial finish line" toward which many of us struggle, often doing work we dislike until we reach a predetermined retirement age and the ensuing mirage of leisure and joy.[24] Anthony explains that the whole notion of "retirement" is a vestige of the industrial age—when we traded grueling manual labor for wages—and makes little sense for today's knowledge workers. Anthony notes that what brings us durable joy is anything that *creates meaning for ourselves* and *provides benefits to others*.

Unfortunately, the modern paradigm deprives many retirees of that happiness by turning them into idle consumers. Under such conditions, they abandon the hero's journey and, often unknowingly, drift day by day into what the historian and National Book Award winner Christopher Lasch calls the decadent and self-indulgent "culture of narcissism."[25] Unable or unwilling to identify and devote themselves to a cause larger than their own egotistical gratifications, they soon grow dissatisfied and unhappy.

Not only is such drifting spiritually and personally corrosive, but it also hastens our physical decline. Anthony recalls a conversation with a gerontologist at the Mayo Clinic who clarifies this cascade: "A life of total *ease* is two steps removed from a life of total *disease*: The first step is that [retirees] get bored, the second step is that they grow pessimistic, and finally they get ill." As the stoic philosophers well knew, the single-minded pursuit of our own pleasure inevitably leaves us, like a drug addict, enslaved to a desire that's both impossible to slake and profoundly unhealthy.

The scientific literature bears this point out. The National Bureau of Economic Research, for example, concludes that, as compared

---

24 Mitch Anthony, *The New Retirementality: Planning Your Life and Living Your Dreams ... at Any Age You Want* (Hoboken, New Jersey: Wiley, fifth edition, 2020).

25 Christopher Lasch, *The Culture of Narcissism: American Life in An Age of Diminishing Expectations* (New York: W. W. Norton and Company, 1979).

with those who continue to work at something they enjoy, "complete retirement leads to a 5-16 percent increase in difficulties associated with mobility and daily activities, a 5-6 percent increase in illness conditions, and 6-9 percent decline in mental health, over an average post-retirement period of six years. Models indicate that the effects tend to operate through lifestyle changes, including declines in physical activity and social interactions."[26] The authors also note that the adverse effects may be more pronounced following mandatory retirement. Either way, those who retire to an idealized but vaguely defined life of leisure often find themselves facing an existential crisis for which they are ill-prepared.

The loss of deep personal relationships can be especially pernicious. How happy can you be if your primary social circle consists of the same three people who make up your golf foursome several times each week and with whom you have the same predictable conversations about political trivia and your putting woes? As Chris Crowley notes, "Staying emotionally connected … turns out to be a biological imperative, a critical part of the good life, and a real challenge as we age…. We evolved as social pack animals…. It's not a choice. Our core survival depends on being part of a group."[27] Mark Danzey quotes a sixty-five-year-old client who makes a related point in seven ominous words: "There is no lonely like retired lonely."[28]

---

26   Dhaval Dave, Inas Rashad, and Jasmina Spasojevic, "The Effects of Retirement on Physical and Mental Health Outcomes," *National Bureau of Economics Research Working Paper 12123*, March 2006.

27   Chris Crowley and Henry Lodge, *Younger Next Year: A Guide to Living Like 50 Until You're 80 and Beyond* (New York: Workman Publishing Company, 2005).

28   Quoted from my *Money and Meaning* podcast, Episode 3, 2021, "How to Create Meaning in Retirement."

FROM ACT 1 TO ACT 2

Few of us change course willingly. Once we start down a path, momentum tends to carry us along in the same direction as if we were being driven by Newton's first law: an object in motion tends to stay in motion unless another force acts upon it. A lucky few of us may course-correct before a moment of crisis, but most of us live by the old maxim, "If it ain't broke, don't fix it."

But everything eventually breaks. How we react to that break defines the rest of our lives. Instead of pushing mindlessly or forlornly forward at crisis point *A*, those who will complete the hero's journey must reconsider their path, connect (or reconnect) to their divine purpose, take corrective action, and, often with the help of a guide, begin another and more profound S curve—one driven not by their egos but by their true selves.

As Paulo Coelho says, "When we least expect it, life sets us a challenge to test our courage and willingness to change; ... there is no point in pretending that nothing has happened or in saying that we are not yet ready. The challenge will not wait. Life does not look back."[29]

Rather than dishearteningly dragging out Act 1 across the dead end of arc AB, the hero pursues a more meaningful Act 2 ascent on arc AC. Note that this ascent generally begins with a period of reflection and reevaluation, which I've labeled "preparation for Act 2" and which involves an interval of learning and capability building akin to the one that occurs at the beginning of Act 1.

---

29 Paulo Coelho, *The Devil and Miss Prym* (New York: HarperOne, reprint edition, 2007).

Falling Upward

These S curves can recur many times in our lives if we continue to cultivate the heroic spirit. As Richard Rohr points out in his paradoxically titled *Falling Upward*, our ability to rise is contingent on the self-knowledge we gain during our moments of crisis—through the often painful but necessary losses we endure and the clarity that follows—like the vivid, dust-free view of startlingly blue sky revealed only after a harrowing storm.[30] Every glorious arising is prefaced by a period of purposeful introspection in which we must reconfigure our spirits, marshal our resources, and discard some of our comforting illusions if we are to prove equal to the new test.

When we come face-to-face with some unexpected and unwelcome challenge, however, most of us are tempted to follow the example of Ulysses when he briefly resists Zeus's call to join the battle against the Trojans. Given Zeus's position atop the Greek pantheon, Ulysses is literally rejecting his God-given purpose. In his hesitancy we recognize our own deep and unheroic resistance to confronting the necessary ordeals in our own lives, whatever the long-term negative consequences for us and others. W. H. Auden describes this resistance brilliantly: "We would rather be ruined than changed. We would rather die in our dread than climb the cross of the moment and let our illusions die."[31]

What marks the hero is a willingness to confront this dread and destroy those illusions. Our tribulations provide clarity, strip away childish innocence and naivete, and replace them with more durable qualities. Think of crises you've gone through. Didn't they help you distinguish what was important from what was trivial, what was sacred

---

30   Richard Rohr, *Falling Upward: Spirituality for the Two Halves of Life* (San Francisco, California: Jossey-Bass Inc., 2011).

31   W. H. Auden, *The Age of Anxiety* (New York: Random House, 1947).

from what was profane? When your child is ill, do you worry about checking the Twitter feed that has obsessed you throughout the past year? Don't your truest and closest friends separate themselves from your mere acquaintances during your life's most difficult passages?

Consider how often the hero's nobility reveals itself only in the face of a crisis. In the *Iliad*, Achilles must endure the death of Patroclus before he stops sulking in his tent, takes up arms, confronts Hector, and fulfills his destiny on the battlefield. Dorothy must hold in mind her desire to return to Kansas before she contends with the Wicked Witch of the West. Without the suffering of being removed from her loved ones, would she have found the courage to face those flying monkeys and their sinister commander? The tornado that drops her into Oz calls forth her character and integrity, which may never have found expression without the unwelcome trial.

> *Every crisis is an opportunity for the growth and insight we need to complete the hero's journey.*

Every crisis is an opportunity for the growth and insight we need to complete the hero's journey. Only what is reliable can survive the stress test we endure at such moments. All that's superficial is stripped away. Like a knight emerging from a harsh series of battles, we grow stronger with each challenge and emerge better prepared to face whatever metaphorical dragons stand in our way.

As the English mystic Mother Julian of Norwich wrote in the 1300s, any expectation that we can avoid these dragons or the hero's journey is pure folly: "If there is anywhere on earth a lover of God who is always kept safe, I know nothing of it, for it was not shown to me. But this was shown: that in falling and rising again we are always kept in that same precious love."[32]

---

32   Julian of Norwich, *Revelations of Divine Love* (Oxford: Oxford University Press, 2015).

Having examined the *meaning* side of the hero's journey in this chapter, I'll now turn to the equally important and more pragmatic *money* side in chapter 5, giving special attention to the hero's economic challenges and to the importance of a trustworthy guide.

CHAPTER 5

VUCA, Finances, and the Hero's Guide

Things in life will not always run smoothly. Sometimes we will be rising toward the heights—then all will seem to reverse itself and start downward. The great fact to remember is that the trend of civilization itself is forever upward; that a line drawn through the middle of the peaks and the valleys of the centuries always has an upward trend.
—FRANKLIN D. ROOSEVELT, INAUGURAL ADDRESS, JANUARY 20, 1945[33]

A VUCA World

When my son was a teenager, we visited the Dialogue in the Dark exhibition.[34] Here blind guides lead visitors through various exhibits

---

33   Franklin Delano Roosevelt, *The Inaugural Addresses of Franklin Delano Roosevelt* (Worcester, Massachusetts: Achille J. St. Onge, 1945).

34   See https://www.dialogue-se.com/what-we-do/dialogue-in-the-dark/.

in absolute darkness. The experience gave us a sense of how stressful life can be without the orienting input from our eyes. Without a guide, our stress would have been magnified exponentially. We'd have been wandering dangerously, ill-prepared through what some describe as a VUCA world. VUCA stands for volatility, uncertainty, complexity, and ambiguity. Borrowing from the leadership theories of Warren Bennis and Burton Nanus,[35] the US Army War College introduced the concept in 1987 to describe the new and disorderly paradigm that began to emerge at the end of the Cold War.[36] The four components of the acronym may be easier to grasp with a visual.

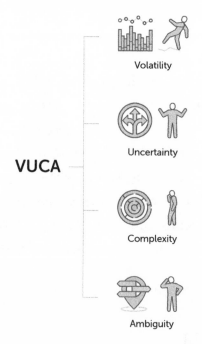

Figure 5.1 A volatile, uncertain, complex, and ambiguous world.

35 Warren Bennis and Burt Nanus, *Leaders: Strategies for Taking Charge* (New York: Harpers Business, second edition, 2007).

36 US Army Heritage and Education Center, "Who first originated the term VUCA (Volatility, Uncertainty, Complexity and Ambiguity)?" May 7, 2018. See https://usawc. libanswers.com/faq/84869.

For my purposes, the concept of VUCA helps clarify the confusing array of financial challenges facing those in the mid to late stages of their careers. Gone are the simpler days when many of us could rely on a pension from our employer and the confident support of government programs such as Social Security and Medicare as we moved into the second and third acts of our lives. In most cases my heroes must manage money challenges on their own. And in most cases, they also lack the specialized knowledge to successfully negotiate this volatile, uncertain, complex, and ambiguous terrain without the help of a guide.

To this point our focus has been primarily on the *meaning* component of the hero's journey. In this chapter we'll shift our attention to equally important questions of *means*—the hero's financial challenges. More specifically we'll focus on the monetary goals all heroes share, the obstacles to achieving those goals, the qualities essential to a guide, the need for a plan capable of adapting to the vagaries of a VUCA environment, and a call to action in which the heroes who implement that plan triumphantly complete their journeys.

Throughout I'll emphasize the essential and complementary relationship between means and meaning. For just as the legendary King Arthur cannot fulfill his divine destiny until he takes possession of the bejeweled sword Excalibur, so my heroes cannot fulfill their true calling unless they are armed and fortified with the financial freedom to live meaningful and abundant lives—in terms they uniquely define.

The Hero's Financial Goals

In the mid to late stages of their careers, all my heroes share a number of goals that require a reliable source of income. Obviously the precise amount will vary. If your true self finds its clearest expression piloting a yacht around the Mediterranean, making yearly donations to help Doctors Without Borders eradicate malaria, or putting your ten grandchildren through college, you're going to require substantial sums of money.

But even if your inspired purpose involves retreating to a quiet cabin in the Appalachian Mountains for a spartan life of inward contemplation, you'll still need to pay for the cabin, buy food, keep up with your electricity bills, and visit a dentist if you slip off your meditation cushion and chip a tooth. As a great sage once said, "There has never yet been a philosopher who could endure a toothache patiently, even though they all write as if they had risen above human suffering and misfortune."[37] Whatever your dreams, inadequate means—and untreated toothaches—will smother their full expression. There's simply no way around that.

All heroes want the freedom to pursue and fulfill their Act 2 goals, to begin the new S curve we discussed in the last chapter. They want the "abundant life" described in John 10:10. They want clarity and peace. They want to take care of the people who matter to them. And they want their friends and neighbors to see them as responsible members of their community—as people who honor their personal commitments, social obligations, and financial duties. But none of these tasks are simple in a VUCA world.

The Hero's Six Financial Challenges

Perhaps the greatest of all Greek heroes, Hercules had to complete twelve "labors" before he could retire in security and avoid the murderous wrath of the goddess Hera. These tasks included slaying a

---

37   William Shakespeare, *Much Ado About Nothing*, Act 5, Scene 1 from *The Riverside Shakespeare* (New York: Houghton Mifflin Company, 1973).

lion, decapitating a multiheaded hydra, and subduing the ferocious dog Cerberus, who guards the gates of the underworld. My heroes' challenges may be less numerous and dramatic, but overcoming them is every bit as important to their long-term well-being. Although we'll examine all of these issues more deeply in part 3 of this book, a quick overview will be helpful here to round out the basic arc of the hero's journey and clarify the importance of finding a knowledgeable guide to help negotiate this difficult terrain.

1. *Markets aren't cheap / returns could be lower.* Those who approach Act 2 as if the scenery from Act 1 will remain in place may be in for a rude and disoriented awakening. That stocks may have earned high returns in the past is no guarantee that they will continue to do so in the future. Just as Hercules would have been in grave danger had he approached the hydra with the same weapon he used on the lion, so my heroes run enormous financial risks if their long-term security requires that history repeat itself.

2. *Interest rates and bond yields are historically low.* Those who count on traditionally "safe and reliable" investments may find themselves on a paradoxically dangerous path in a VUCA environment. Just as Dorothy must recognize "I'm not in Kansas anymore" when the talking apple tree in Oz slaps her hand, so my heroes must recognize that what worked for an earlier generation may not work for them.

3. *We're living longer.* Modern Americans live twenty-five years longer than they did a century ago.[38] Clearly that's an enormous sign of progress. But with that progress comes

---

38 Diane Whitmore Schanzenbach, Ryan Nunn, and Lauren Bauer, "The Changing Landscape of American Life Expectancy," *The Hamilton Project*, June 2016.

new kinds of challenges. How do we ensure a high quality of life across that quarter century given that the retirement age has remained relatively constant? How do our heroes structure their savings to ensure that they can live Acts 2 through 5 with the same financial freedom they had in Act 1? We cannot look to the past for answers to these emerging questions. As Klosterman notes, when Germany established a social benefits program for those over sixty-five, the average life expectancy was forty-seven. Living longer may be a nice problem to have, but that doesn't mean that it isn't, at some level, still a problem. If those additional years are marred by penury and suffering, the initial luster of this achievement quickly begins to fade.

4. *Healthcare costs are increasing.* The United States has the best healthcare system in the world, but it's extremely expensive and getting more so. In addition the older our heroes get, the more they spend on healthcare. The Fidelity Retiree Health Care Cost Estimate reports that in 2020, the average retired couple age sixty-five may need about $295,000 saved (after tax) for postretirement healthcare expenses. And Steve Fein-schreiber, senior vice president of the Financial Solutions Group at Fidelity, says, "Health care is creating a 'retirement cost gap' for many pre-retirees. Many people assume Medicare will cover all … health care cost in retirement, but it doesn't. We estimate that about 15% of the average retiree's annual expenses will be used for health care-related expenses, including Medicare premiums and out-of-pocket expenses."[39] One of our aging heroes' unavoidable challenges

---

39   "How to plan for rising health care costs," *Fidelity Viewpoints*, August 3, 2020.

is how to prepare for these steep financial challenges as they move into the second and third acts of their lives.

5. *Social Security, Medicare, and other government programs may not be able to provide the level of support they have in the past.* Simply as a matter of shifting demographics, those who are counting on traditional forms of government support in Act 2 and beyond may be in for unpleasant shock. To put the matter bluntly, the number of program *beneficiaries* is rapidly outpacing the number of program *contributors*. When Social Security was developed, people lived about seven years after retirement, so the government didn't need a lot of capital to fund that period. Today the interval has increased to roughly thirty years. That's a long promise to pay, especially when you consider that seniors are the fastest-growing part of the population. It comes down to a simple math problem: we have fewer workers and many more retirees, more passengers and fewer people manning the oars. The hero's plan of action must account for this new and ever-changing reality.

6. *An unprepared, underfunded, or unguided hero may make behavioral mistakes in pursuing the illusion of safety.* My heroes have lived through two scary downturns in a little more than a decade: the tech bubble bursting from 1999 to 2002 and the great financial crisis from 2007 to 2009. As a result they're feeling beaten up and anxious. Those emotions don't provide a solid foundation for making astute investment decisions that will see them past the opening act in their lives.

But because they can't rely on the company pensions that served their parents, my heroes are going to have to make these decisions—and make them in a VUCA environment.

They can't count on anyone but themselves to secure their financial future. Unfortunately, in trying to avoid risk, they're often unconsciously increasing it. How? By putting their money in asset classes that almost certainly won't provide the rising income stream they need to see them through the rest of their lives. And there's no safety net here. They don't get a do-over. If they make decisions based on fear, they're running an enormous risk of outliving their money.

And as we'll discuss in part 3, the media preys on and increases these fears, encouraging already confused heroes to make panicked and unwise decisions that simply compound their problems. Like an inexperienced pilot entering a cloudbank, their sense of precisely where they are and what they should do becomes unreliable, and the risk of a crash increases dramatically.

Finding a Guide

Just as the disoriented Dante needs Virgil to restore his sense of perspective, just as Sylvester Stallone's distraught Rocky Balboa needs Apollo Creed to help him prepare for his rematch with Clubber Lang (i.e., Mr. T), so twenty-first-century heroes need a financial guide to lead them safely through the VUCA conditions that jeopardize their long-term safety and happiness.

How do you find a reliable guide as opposed to a charlatan? Two qualities are essential: empathy and authority. All effective guides need to understand the hero's problem—often because they have faced the same problem themselves. They also need expertise in how to solve that problem. As a former opponent, Creed understands and sympathizes with Rocky's frustration; as a fighter expert in dealing with brawling foes like Lang, Creed is also ideally positioned to reshape Rocky's style in a way that will help him reverse his previous loss.

Although I can't prepare you to fight the heavyweight champion, I'm writing this book because I've faced (and am still facing) the challenges you face. I can empathize with your plight because it's mine as well. And while you may have authority as a doctor, a lawyer, an engineer, a teacher, an entrepreneur, or in some other calling, I've had thirty-six years of experience helping clients move successfully from Act 1 to the remainder of their lives. I'm certainly not the only one who can help you make this transition, but you need to work with someone who has a proven track record in facing money and meaning challenges.

Next, the guide needs to clarify what one of my own coaches, Dan Sullivan, creator of Strategic Coach®, calls The D.O.S.® tool: What are your *dangers, opportunities, strengths*? What are your current financial resources? How do they align with your long-term goals? These questions are all person-specific. Beware of any guide who simply tries to apply a fixed formula to all his clients. You aren't a robot looking for an algorithm. You're a complex human being with complex challenges and desires. Trustworthy guides need to take the time to understand your unique needs and objectives.

Only then can they take the next step: developing a plan tailored to secure the financial means required for you to live the meaningful life you've defined. And that plan should offer you options—because there is almost certainly more than one correct answer about how to secure the financial means to live a meaningful life. I once had the privilege of seeing a presentation by the great *National Geographic* photographer Dewitt Jones. When he displayed a photo of Machu Picchu, my reaction was that no image of the site could possibly be more moving. Had you told me I could have one picture from his collection to hang on my office wall, I'd immediately have asked for this one. That feeling lasted until I saw the second photo of the exact same landscape from a different perspective, and it was even more spectacular than the first. My point here is that the guide who provides a single plan—no matter how brilliant it may seem at first—may be shortchanging his clients. Only when they review multiple options are they in a position to understand the trade-offs and possibilities.

Once the plan is crafted, the guide issues a call to action, which turns the abstraction into a reality. A perfect recipe is no good if you never bake the cake. So the guide must inspire the hero to set forth—and to do so with clarity and confidence.

Whatever travails our heroes suffer, they ultimately recognize that the trend of their journey is always and ever upward toward financially-free and meaningful lives.

What's crucial here, however, is that the guide accompany you on the journey. You're not enlisting him to make a plan and leave. Why? Because as you begin, the terrain will change, new challenges will arise, your spirits may flag, and your circumstances or objectives may shift. Act 2 will give way to Acts 3, 4, and 5. So the plan needs to be altered as you go. That's why your financial guide must be passionate about ongoing collaboration to assess progress and make the inevitable course corrections required in a VUCA world.

Through this process heroes transform from those who felt uncertain about whether they had the means to complete their journeys to those eager to take on new challenges, to echo Ulysses' heartening words as he sets out for a second time from Ithaca, "To strive, to seek, to find, and not to yield."[40] Circling back to the FDR quote with which we opened this chapter, we can say that whatever travails our heroes suffer, they ultimately recognize that the trend of their journey is always and ever upward toward financially-free and meaningful lives. I'll explore this idea more fully in chapter 15, when I make the case for the wisdom of living as a "rational optimist."

As we move on now to part 2, I'll serve as a guide to the deep discovery that is an essential prelude to forming an individual action plan and embarking on your own hero's journey.

---

40   Alfred, Lord Tennyson, "Ulysses," *Selected Poems* (New York: Penguin Classics, 2008).

PART 2

PART 2

The Money and Meaning Experience[41]

---

41 Chapters six through eight contain, in part, materials from the *Money and Meaning Experience Workshop* I periodically offer my clients.

CHAPTER 6

Getting Clear—Who Are You? Why Are You Here?

We come into this world with a specific, personal destiny. We have a job to do, a calling to enact, a self to become. We are who we are from the cradle, and we're stuck with it. Our job in this lifetime is not to shape ourselves into some ideal we imagine we ought to be, but to find out who we already are and become it.

—STEVEN PRESSFIELD[42]

Shifting Gears

Having talked in *general* terms about the *theoretical* journey all of us take in moving beyond the opening act of our lives, we're now going to get *personal* and *practical*. We've clarified the broad pattern, but how do you translate those overviews and archetypes to your specific circumstances?

---

42 Stephen Pressfield, *The War of Art: Break Through the Blocks and Win Your Inner Creative Battles* (New York: Black Irish Entertainment, 2002).

I've emphasized that we all have unique gifts and an individual God-given purpose, but neither of these comes printed out in bold type on our birth certificates or our college diplomas. We each have to make these difficult discoveries on our own. It's all well and good to say that, like Ulysses, we'll go through a series of challenges on the road to a life-altering insight, but the Trojan War ended more than three thousand years ago. Sharpening a sword in the garage isn't a viable strategy for those entering the mid to late stages of our careers in the 2020s.

In this chapter then, my focus will shift to self-discovery. Throughout I'll share actionable information based on what I've learned through years of coaching and working with clients. I'll also draw on resources from various organizations and programs that have enabled me to define and enact the various S curves in my own hero's journey.[43] My aim is to help you look inward and identify your foundational desires and capabilities so you can better understand precisely who you are, what role you were born to fulfill, where your fundamental talents reside, and how you can begin to cultivate and apply those talents in ways that create value for others and meaning for yourself.

City Slickers

In talking to clients about the quest for self-knowledge, I often refer to the 1991 movie *City Slickers*, in which Billy Crystal and two other characters rather pathetically try to combat their midlife crises by engaging in reckless and artificial adventures, such as running with the bulls in Pamplona, Spain. After Crystal is humiliatingly gored in his

---

43   I have no financial affiliations with any of these organizations and programs, nor do I claim to have developed any of the resources I cite. I'm merely recommending strategies that have proven effective for me.

GETTING CLEAR—WHO ARE YOU? WHY ARE YOU HERE?

backside, his wife snidely but accurately refers to these forced and self-conscious escapades as "desperate attempts to cling to your youth." Pursuing ultimately empty thrills unrelated to their true selves, the comically deluded protagonists are clearly stuck in their Act 1 lives: repeating a formula that repeatedly fails.

Stagnating in a job he has come to loathe, feeling that he's wasting his life, telling his wife he feels "lost" and "trapped," Crystal attempts to change his trajectory through a clichéd "old West" adventure: his friends celebrate his birthday with a gift that will allow him to participate in a two-week cattle drive from New Mexico to Colorado. Certainly getting back in touch with nature and mingling with hard-working, old-school, no-nonsense rustics will allow him to imbibe, as if through osmosis, the wisdom he needs to live a happier life. As the drive begins, one of his friends looks across the landscape and confidently proclaims that "out there are all the answers."

Viewers are justifiably skeptical. Isn't this just another performative gesture, another trophy-like experience he can brag about to his friends? Shouldn't he be looking inward for answers about what changes might make his life meaningful? Isn't the notion of the hardscrabble yet wise cowboy as guru just another romantic Hollywood cliché?

Not entirely. True, the terrifying trail boss, Jack Palance, ticks all the roughneck, macho boxes of the most melodramatic John Wayne or Clint Eastwood character. But he also sees the city slickers for what they are. In the movie's most memorable scene, Palance cuts through the pretense. He calls Crystal the typical overworked urbanite who spends fifty weeks tying himself into knots and then expects to solve all his problems by putting on a ten-gallon hat and living out a two-week fantasy while rubbing shoulders with cowpokes. The secret of life, he cryptically tells Crystal, is "one thing," and if a person knows that, nothing else really matters. When the puzzled but hopeful Crystal asks what that thing is, Palance responds like a Zen master: "That's what *you've* got to figure out."

Palance's point is clear: we can't offload the work of self-discovery to someone else. By definition, the nature of personal insight is ... *personal*. Many of us have problems late in Act 1, however, when we realize we've allowed other people to chart the course of our whole lives. Like Crystal, we've never discovered our "one thing." Consciously or not, we've delegated that task to others.

Your Self-Excavation

The exercises that follow are intended as an excavation project, clearing away the inessential debris from your life so you can unearth your often obscured fundamentals, identify your neglected foundational priorities, and discover your "one thing."

WHAT IS YOUR WHY?[44]

I had a friend who went to law school, studied hard, paid a fortune in tuition, graduated with distinction, and *never* practiced law—or took the bar exam. During that whole period, he was running on automatic pilot, behaving like a robot. He knew precisely *what* he was doing (i.e., getting a law degree), he knew *how* he was doing it (i.e., putting in long hours in the library of a prestigious law school), but somehow he'd never asked himself *why* he was charting this course. Only after the fact did he recognize what had always been obvious:

---

44   I've drawn my ideas for this section from Simon Sinek's *Start with Why: How Great Leaders Inspire Everyone to Take Action* (New York: Portfolio, 2011). See also his inspiring TED Talk at https://www.ted.com/talks/simon_sinek_how_great_leaders_inspire_action?language=en.

he had no true calling to be a lawyer, he did not enjoy his studies, and his primary motivation was to please his father.

I cite this example because it perfectly illustrates the pitfalls that await us all unless we begin our hero's journey with a clear sense of *why* we are undertaking it. Unless that *why* relates to "What makes you come alive?"[45] the entire enterprise will be misbegotten. *What* and *how* answers are meaningless unless they emerge from our foundational purpose in life. Although the point may seem obvious, almost all of us spend part of our lives solving *what* and *how* questions untethered from any elemental *why*. Recall my own earlier example as a young man driving a Volvo, wearing tailored suits, trying to increase my client base, and so on without any deep sense of why I was in business. Only when I found my *why*—helping clients manage their finances in ways that make their lives more meaningful—did my job provide the satisfaction I'd been seeking from the start. Ironically my *why* turned out to be helping others discover and answer their own *why* questions. The key point here is to begin your hero's journey from the inner circle of this graph and work your way out.

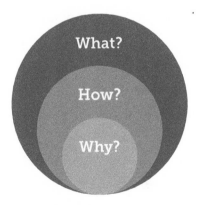

Figure 6.1 Find your purpose

Take a moment here and answer the question "What is my why?" in the space below. Return to this question periodically to update and adjust this answer.

_____

_____

_____

THE THREE GEORGE KINDER QUESTIONS[46]

When I meet with a prospective client, I always begin with three questions: Question one is, "If you suddenly had $30 million in the bank, safe and liquid, how would you live your life?" A lot of people's answers focus on what they'd do for their family—sending their kids to a good college, buying a new home for their parents. Some talk about contributing to causes. Others say they'd want to travel, simply have fun, or quit their job. What's revealing about the question is that it gives us some broad clues about what really matters to the speaker.

Question two is less pleasant: You've lost the $30 million (easy come, easy go!), and you're constrained by whatever your current finances are. You go to the doctor (if you're married, you go with your spouse), who gives you a good news/bad news scenario: you're both going to be in perfect health for the rest of your lives, but you're going to die painlessly five to ten years from today. How would you

---

46 This section draws on two books by George Kinder: *Life Planning for You: How to Design and Deliver the Life of Your Dreams* (Littleton, Massachusetts: Serenity Point Press, 2014) and *The Seven Stages of Money Maturity: Understanding the Spirit and Value of Money in Your Life* (New York: Dell Publishing, reprint edition, 2000).

spend those years? How would you live differently from how you're living today?

In essence I'm asking that clients run a kind of fire drill before the inevitable fire. Again, this helps both the client and me see what's important. As Samuel Johnson once said, "Depend upon it, sir, when a man knows he is to be hanged in a fortnight, it concentrates his mind wonderfully."[47] Kinder's question does something similar—though without the stigma and pain of a public execution! It encourages us to look beyond the comfortable status quo and see the folly of acting as if we were going to live forever. We're unlikely to keep dithering away our lives and postponing what we find important if our tombstones have an engraved end date. Of course, we all know in the abstract that we're going to die, but our daily actions often seem uninformed by that knowledge. Question two often helps us snap out of that stupor.

Question three is even more daunting: now you go to the same doctor, but your life span is reduced to twenty-four hours. The real question here isn't so much how will you spend your last day, but "What did you *not* get to see or experience that saddens you or that stands out as a regret?" Again, this question helps us home in on essentials. Most people speak of not getting to see their children or grandchildren grow up. The missed trip to the Amazon tends to fade in importance. And I've never heard anyone say, "I wish I'd stayed at the office longer!" or "Man, I wish I'd finished that project for my boss!"

I encourage you to put down the book at this point, sit quietly by yourself or with your spouse, and work through these questions. Don't rush. Take the time to consider them thoroughly. Write down your answers. Over the next few days, update them as new thoughts arise.

---

47   James Boswell, *The Life of Samuel Johnson* (New York: Penguin Classics, 2009).

This isn't an easy task. But by the time you finish, your self-excavation project will be well under way.

1. If you had $30 million, how would you live your life?

_____

_____

_____

2. If you knew you would die in five to ten years, how would you change your life?

_____

_____

_____

3. If you knew you would die in twenty-four hours, what would you regret not getting to experience or do?

_____

_____

_____

BEGIN WITH THE END IN MIND[48]

At what age are you going to die?

Dan Sullivan asks this provocative question in his book *My Plan for Living to 156: Imaginatively Extend Your Lifetime to Transform How You Live in the Present*. Although none of us knows the answer to this question, when asked, an age often pops into our heads based on what we consider a full life. Sullivan goes on to encourage us to think about the ideal qualities you want to possess at the end of your life physically, mentally, financially, with relationships, and with regard to your purpose. What are the qualities that would make for a perfect exit? So, for example, you might say, "I want to be *physically* fit enough to play with my grandchildren, *mentally* acute enough to complete the *New York Times* daily crossword puzzle, *financially* secure enough to maintain my current standard of living, and engaged in loving *relationships* with my family and friends—as well as having an overall self-assessment that I'm still living a full life." Why not put the book down and spend a few minutes thinking about this for yourself?

No one ever answers that they'd like to be in poor health, mentally unstable, broke, with no friends and no purpose. Given the positive outcomes you envisioned and that these correlate with longer life expectancies, ask yourself, "If I had the qualities I just specified, might I not live longer than my initial estimate?" How much longer might you live? When I did this exercise for the first time, I optimistically guessed I might live an additional fifteen years.

Spend a few minutes thinking about your own extra years and the joy they would allow you to experience. Ideally what would you like

---

48   This section merges ideas from Steven Covey's *The 7 Habits of Highly Effective People* (New York: Simon and Schuster, 2004) and Dan Sullivan's *My Plan For Living To 156: Imaginatively Extend Your Lifetime to Transform How You Live in the Present* (Powell, Ohio: Author Academy Elite, 2019). To learn more, visit strategiccoach.com/go/156.

to be doing during those extra years? Maybe you'd take your grandkids to Disneyland or visit Rome or learn to speak Italian. Again, take your time. Allow yourself to feel elated. After all, you've just been granted (literally) a new lease on life!

Once you've finished that, you're ready for the key questions: "What are you waiting for? Why do you need those extra years to revel in the activities that matter to you? Why don't you do them now?"

VALUES CLARIFICATION EXERCISE

Circle ten to twelve values you prize from the following list. Consider them for a few minutes, and then place a check mark next to the top five. Continue your reflection until you are ready to list the top three—in order of importance—under the *You* column. Then follow the example for "Learning" by filling in your *Beliefs* about each value and the *Actions* you associate with it. Post this list somewhere you will see it each day to help keep your actions aligned with your values and beliefs.

I redid the exercise while writing this book and found subtle but important shifts in the values I selected and the beliefs and actions I'd written out several years ago. I thus recommend that you reinterrogate yourself from time to time so that your answers align with your ever-changing life circumstances.

Figure 6.2 Values clarification.

Possible choices of values—please feel free to choose values not on this list.

Accountability	Fairness	Mission focus
Achievement	Faith	Open communication
Ambition	Family	Openness
Balance (home/work)	Financial stability	Perseverance
Career	Forgiveness	Personal fulfillment
Clarity	Friendships	Personal growth
Commitment	Future generations	Power
Community involvement	Generosity	Purpose
Compassion	Health	Quality
Competence	Honesty	Respect
Conflict resolution	Humility	Responsibility

Continuing learning	Humor/Fun	Risk-taking
Cooperation	Independence	Safety
Courage	Integrity	Self-confidence
Creativity	Initiative	Self-discipline
Dependability	Intuition	Success
Efficiency	Job security	Trust
Enthusiasm	Listening	Vision
Environmental awareness	Learning	Wisdom
Ethics	Logic	
Excellence	Making a difference	

YOU	BELIEFS	ACTIONS
Learning	*"I want to be a lifelong learner. All life experiences are an opportunity to learn and grow."*	*"I will read twelve books per year."* *"I will research the history of places I travel."*
1.		
2.		
3.		

Your Unique Ability®49

We can all think of many activities at which, no matter how diligently we might practice or study, we will always be incompetent. Not everyone is cut out to be an athlete, a musician, a mathematician, and so on. We might *want* to excel in these spheres, but devoting our lives to them is a recipe for frustration. This is also true for those activities at which hard work would only raise us to a level of basic competence. They simply aren't our true calling.

To pursue a career, a mission, or an avocation that we are intellectually gifted for but psychologically repelled by is as foolhardy as to pursue something for which we lack talent.

We can also think of activities at which we might excel, but simply don't enjoy. We might have the natural gifts necessary to earn admittance to a top medical school and become a first-rate physician, but perhaps we loathe the idea of meeting with sick people each day. To pursue a career, a mission, or an avocation that we are intellectually gifted for but psychologically repelled by is as foolhardy as to pursue something for which we lack talent.

What we need to identify are those activities where our passion and our talents intersect. Dan Sullivan has created the concept of Unique Ability®, and he describes how when we find this sweet spot, we can work for hours without any sense of drudgery. Indeed, we often find that we have more energy when we finish than when we started. That's a sign that we've tapped into our true calling, our

---

49   Unique Ability® is a registered trademark, protected by copyright and an integral concept of the Strategic Coach® Inc.

God-given purpose. The goal is to try to spend most of our time in those areas and rely on others for the tasks at which we either don't excel or don't enjoy.

TOOLS FOR FINDING YOUR UNIQUE GIFTS

I've found four tools especially helpful when working with people struggling to find their true calling. No doubt you can find other resources that will work similarly well—and I encourage you to seek them out. As an excellent starting point, however, I suggest you explore the following, all of which complement the material already presented.

Begin with the Life Assessment Profile designed by Michael Hyatt, coauthor of *Living Forward*[50]—a book I also recommend. Hyatt's online assessment is free and takes just fifteen minutes to complete. His materials provide "simple but proven principles to help you stop drifting, design a Life Plan with the end in mind, and chart a path that will take you there. And you can work the process in just one day." See https://www.livingforwardassessment.com.

The Kolbe Concept˙ is the best tool I've ever seen for helping people uncover their natural strengths. The Kolbe methodology will help you identify your individual instinctive (and best) way of solving problems. Though the service is not free, the modest cost is, in my experience, well worth the investment. Visit kolbe.com for more details. I would especially encourage the readers to explore the Kolbe A™ Index, a link that appears on the kolbe.com home page.

---

50   Michael Hyatt and Daniel Harkavy, *Living Forward: A Proven Plan to Stop Drifting and Get the Life You Want* (Ada, Michigan: Baker Books, 2016).

Consider working through the Unique Ability® 2.0: Discovery workbook from the Strategic Coach. This book and workbook will help you get clear on your Unique Ability®.[51]

You may also want to take the CliftonStrengths Assessment. The reports and guides that flow from this assessment will help give you an *aha!* moment as you experience new ways to understand what makes you unique and to better aim your strengths at success. Learn more at https://www.gallup.com/cliftonstrengths/.

Finally, I've recently retaken and benefited enormously from the Enneagram. You can access it in many places. I found great value in the RHETI® test offered by the Enneagram Institute®. This test will help you understand your unique profile across nine interconnected personality types (e.g., achiever, peacemaker, challenger). Learn more at www.enneagraminstitute.com.

Act 2 Reflection

Having explored your *why*, clarified your values, and assessed your Unique Ability®, take a moment to write down the three greatest obstacles or potential pitfalls that might cause you to recapitulate Act 1 in the coming years rather than enabling Acts 2 through 5 to transcend all you've previously done and serve as the vibrant and rewarding culmination of your life's drama.

1. _____

_____

---

51   Visit https://uniqueability.com/the-book/ for more information.

2. _____

   _____

3. _____

   _____

In the next chapter, we'll begin to address these challenges as we talk about the stage on which you can apply the self-knowledge you've discovered on the previous pages.

CHAPTER 7

Finding Your Act 2 Stage

For many successful people, midlife is the first time they address emotional issues that have been buried on their rush toward accomplishment.... We run the risk of missing much of the growth and blessing at midlife if we rush off only to more accomplishments, even though they may be eternally significant accomplishments.

—LLOYD REEB[52]

Be Discerning

Having clarified your unique values, passions, and talents in chapter 6, we now turn our attention to the stage on which you will perform your second act. The chief pitfall at this point is to rush back into action before you've studied and compared various roles, fully evaluated and tested your options, and found activities that you'll enjoy because they align with what makes you come alive. Too often, however, the desire simply to get busy pushes us to make premature and unwise

---

52 Lloyd Reeb and Bill Wellons, *Unlimited Partnership: Igniting a Marketplace Leader's Journey to Significance* (Nashville, Tennessee: B&H Publishing Group, 2007).

choices we'll later regret. Similarly, many of us feel guilty if we aren't immediately piling up accomplishments—as if Act 2 were just an extension of Act 1, as if we were still college students selecting a path with our eyes blindered, as if we'd come this far in our hero's journey and grown no wiser.

This chapter will help you avoid these compulsive and self-defeating actions in three ways:

By encouraging you to remain fully conscious and discerning as you select your new roles rather than shifting into automatic pilot.

By helping you see that taking the time to consider your options is not malingering or dithering away your life; it's the essential opening scene to a rewarding Act 2, the necessary foreground to your next S curve, a step you cannot skip.

By providing exercises and resources, as in the previous chapter, that encourage you to slow down and explore the full array of your possibilities.[53] These can range from spending time with your grandchildren to serving a nonprofit cause you are passionate about. But depending on your financial situation or on what gives you joy, you might also want to spend all or some of Act 2 in the for-profit world. Keep in mind that you needn't confine yourself to a single role. My only caution is that you not approach this life change with the mindset of an "achievement addict" and take on so many potentially rewarding responsibilities that they form a cumulative burden. You might enjoy a round of golf on occasion, but if you schedule thirty-six holes per day, your enthusiasm (and your shoulder sockets) will quickly break down in misery.

---

53   Again, I have no financial affiliations with any of the organizations who developed these exercises and resources, and although I have adapted them to my own purposes and audience, I make no claim to their originality. I'm simply modifying and sharing content that has proven useful in guiding my clients.

On What Stage Will I Perform My Next Act?[54]

In the following table, describe three widely varying stages on which your talents and passions might allow you to flourish in Act 2. You needn't include the stages I've listed.

Stage 1, for example, might be service-oriented, so you could write something like "Annual church mission trip to Costa Rica," "Sitting on a nonprofit board," "Becoming a volunteer for adult literacy and teaching someone to read," or whatever appeals to you.

Stage 2 could be family related. Keep in mind that there is no taboo against simply having fun. My son and I, for example, have recently taken up fly-fishing. So I might write "Monthly fishing trip with Nick."

Stage 3 might be a for-profit activity such as "Consulting in my industry" or, like me, "Continue in my current business, but connect it to my higher purpose."

When you've finished that, put the book down for a bit and spend some time considering the pros and cons of each option you've listed. Then complete the right-hand side of the table. This exercise will get your exploratory juices flowing and give you a good first approximation of the broad possibilities for staging Act 2. Failure to consider the full spectrum of your interests and options at the outset is a recipe for frustration.

Keep in mind that this seldom proves to be a linear process. Be prepared to modify these ideas as your life circumstances change. A guide can be extremely helpful at such times.

54　This section is my adaptation of an exercise developed by the Halftime Institute.

Figure 7.1 On what stage might I apply my unique gifts?

STAGE 1	
DESCRIPTION	**REFLECTION**

STAGE 2	
DESCRIPTION	**REFLECTION**

STAGE 3	
DESCRIPTION	**REFLECTION**

Choosing Your Role[55]

In addition to choosing a stage, you also need to think about the role you want to play. Do you need to be the central character? Would you be happier in a supporting role? Even if you want to work behind the scenes, do you aspire to be the director running the whole show, or would you rather be a designer building the stage sets? The promoter developing marketing materials? A fundraiser? A ticket taker? There's only one wrong answer: taking on a role you regret.

To help you answer these questions, look at the following list and circle any of the bullet points that appeal to you. Depending on your needs and desires, you can pursue most of these options in both nonprofit or for-profit arenas.

- *Team member:* Avoid large-scale oversight or policy-making responsibilities, but help fulfill a mission you care about by working in the trenches and performing essential hands-on tasks.

- *Teacher, coach, mentor:* Work directly with individuals or groups to impart one of your skill sets and enrich the lives of others.

- *Communicator, marketer, spokesperson, advocate:* Use your writing, designing, or public speaking skills to promote a cause that inspires you.

- *Researcher, analyst, evaluator:* Develop policies or products vital to an organization, or analyze their impact and thus maximize efficiency.

---

55 This section adapts materials from two sources: Marci Alboher's *The Encore Career Handbook: How to Make a Living and a Difference in the Second Half of Life* (New York: Workman Publishing Company, 2012) and the Halftime Institute (https://halftimeinstitute.org/).

- *Fundraiser:* Help an organization raise the capital it needs to achieve its full potential.

- *Entrepreneur:* Develop a business that creates meaning for you and provides value to others.

- *Board member:* Use your big-picture expertise to help guide an organization.

- *Leader, director:* Use your managerial expertise to guide day-to-day operations for an organization—or a project within an organization.

- *Consultant:* Apply your expertise on an as-needed basis to help organizations set policies that enable them to maximize their efficiency.

- *Silent partner:* Work behind the scenes to help an organization's leader.

- *Other:* _____

From the roles you've circled, list three that you find most intriguing and the first steps you will take to explore them.

1. _____

2. _____

3. _____

Test the Waters

No one with a range of options would relocate to Buenos Aires on the basis of pronouncements in a slick brochure, a Rick Steves travel show, or the recommendation of a friend. You can't know for sure how you'll feel about a city without spending some time there. The same logic applies to your second act plans: before you commit to a new role, you need to schedule the equivalent of an exploratory visit to Argentina.

In essence you're conducting a kind of reverse audition by taking on a limited role to decide if the circumstances that seemed inviting *in the abstract* are *in practice* right for you. Before you sign a five-year Netflix deal, you're going to perform in a single episode to see if you enjoy working with the director, the writer, and the other performers. If all goes well and you feel the organization is a good fit, you can make a longer commitment with your eyes wide open, but if you have reservations, you're under no obligation to continue. You have a time-delimited and above-board exit strategy. And you can use the experience to help readjust your sights and home in on a more rewarding position.

In some cases you may discover that although you are not a good fit for one role, an adjacent position you initially dismissed suits you perfectly. I'm speaking from experience here. When I agreed to become the head coach of my son's fifth-grade football team, I assumed the job would focus primarily on fundamentals: blocking and tackling, getting eleven kids to function as a team, clarifying the responsibilities of an outside linebacker.

Boy was I wrong.

I spent the majority of my time placating parents, arranging for snacks to be delivered to the sidelines, rescheduling practices, and on a host of other details unrelated to the gridiron. But I made an important discovery: the assistant coach was unburdened by these administrative duties. He was showing the boys how to get in a four-point stance, run post patterns, and throw a tight spiral. That's exactly what I wanted to do. Since my agreement was for one season only, I took a wise demotion, became an assistant, and discovered one piece of my Act 2 calling. The key takeaway here is to be discerning: you may need to run a number of trials before you find the position you want.

> *You may need to run a number of trials before you find the position you want.*

A Family Vision[56]

The bounty of opportunities Act 2 presents comes with some challenges as well. If your second act requires relocation and separation from a support network of family and friends, you need to carefully consider alternatives and trade-offs before you finalize the move. Of course, these kinds of challenges are especially acute for couples. If I want to move to Key West to do some fishing and part-time consulting and my wife wants to stay in Georgia to be close to our children and serve as an advocate for a local cause, we have a serious problem. So communication, compromise, and creativity are vital during this period of transition.

I recommend that couples begin by nonjudgmentally inquiring about their Act 2 visions. The results will inevitably fall into one of the following three categories:

1. Their visions are entirely separate.

---

56 This section draws on Lloyd and Linda Reeb's *Halftime for Couples* (Irving, Texas: Halftime Institute, 2012).

2. Their visions overlap: they share some features but not others.

3. Their visions are identical.

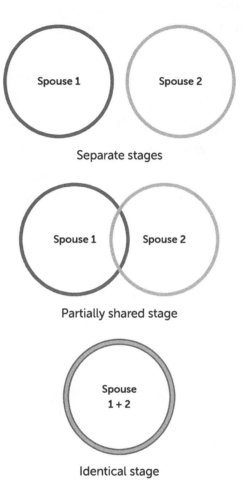

Figure 7.2 Couples model for Act 2 contribution.

None of these is necessarily better than the others, but it's important for couples to understand the differences so they can cope with the specific challenges each presents. Couples on separate stages must guard against drifting apart—becoming so caught up in their individual projects that they lose touch with each other. Building in time to reconnect is essential. Couples on an identical stage face the opposite problem. As the old saying goes, "I married you for better or worse but not for breakfast, lunch, and dinner every day." Here the challenge is to keep from smothering each other—to allow enough space and private time to cultivate your separate identities. Those on a partially shared stage face variations of the previous two challenges: finding the best way to complement each other's overlapping interests and to avoid disappearing into their separate domains.

For those with children (and grandchildren), Act 2 presents a special opportunity to connect in ways that may not have been possible during the frantic, striving stages of Act 1. Take a moment to write down your vision of what an ideal relationship might look like for each family member. And then be sure to budget time for these loved ones as you formulate a plan for the next stage in your life.

In chapter 8 we'll talk about creating the margin you need to launch a successful second act.

Creating Margin and Getting Free

No margin, no mission.

—SISTER IRENE KRAUS, DAUGHTERS OF CHARITY,
ON THE IMPORTANCE OF EFFICIENT FISCAL
MANAGEMENT IN MEETING HER RELIGIOUS
ORDER'S PHILANTHROPIC IDEALS.[57]

Margin and Mission

"Margin" often connotes quite different meanings to financial planners like myself, statisticians calculating error rates, and those formatting a document in Microsoft Word. For our purposes, I like Richard Swenson's definition: "Margin is the space between our load and our limits.... It is something held in reserve for contingencies or

---

57   "No Margin, No Mission: Flying Nuns and Sister Irene Kraus," *Tele-Tracking*, March 20, 2012 (https://www.teletracking.com/resources/no-margin-no-mission-flying-nuns-and-sister-irene-kraus).

unanticipated situations. Margin is the gap between rest and exhaustion, the space between breathing freely and suffocating."[58] It's also the difference between living comfortably and being destitute.

Without adequate margins of time, energy, and money, none of us can fulfill our highest aspirations. Of course, the precise amounts of these variables will always be person- and context-specific: someone attempting to eradicate the malaria parasite from the planet will need greater financial margins than someone trying to increase literacy in a small rural town. But no matter what our calling, we all need to satisfy certain basic needs. Even the stoical Gandhi needed a minimal level of calories to fuel his lofty aims. We all need shelter, healthcare, safety, and love. These are nonnegotiable.

Beyond that we have wants and desires that give our lives meaning. You can't devote your life to mastering the violin unless you can purchase an instrument, hire a teacher, find time to practice, and summon the energy to do so. As Sister Kraus pithily put it, "No margin. No mission."

And if I might add a third emphatic item to her list: "No exceptions."

In this chapter we'll confront that hard truth and clarify how you can *clarify*, *create*, and, equally important, *protect* the margin you need to live your life to the fullest. Following the workshop format of chapters 6 and 7, I'll provide exercises and resources to guide you on this quest. By the time you finish, you'll have a clear sense of both what you need *to do* and what you need *to stop doing* to fulfill your hero's journey.

---

58   Richard Swenson, *Margin: Restoring Emotional, Physical, Financial, and Time Reserves to Overloaded Lives* (Colorado Springs: NavPress, 2004).

Focusing Your Time Efficiently[59]

Most of our daily activities fall into one of the following three time-related categories:

1. *Capacity killers.* Former Google ethicist Tristan Harris says that ideally we want to look back on each day as "time well spent."[60] By that, he doesn't mean that every moment needs to be robotically goal-driven or judged against some spartan code of assembly-line work efficiency. Time spent idly with family or friends can be well spent if it connects us with those we love. But excruciating hours in a dentist's chair getting a dreaded root canal are also well spent because they protect our health.

   By "capacity killers," I'm referring to time devoted to activities that are neither productive nor enjoyable: meetings with no purpose, YouTube sessions whose chief aim is to distract us from a matter that needs our attention, busy work that we drift toward to avoid more taxing and important matters, trivial and distracting texts, emails, phone calls, and face-to-face exchanges. These and many other avoidance strategies can allow us to drift unmindfully through a day we'll look back on with regret—as time wasted. In later sections of this chapter, I'll outline strategies to reduce or eliminate distractions that can rob our lives of joy.

---

59   In this section, I've adapted ideas from Steven Covey's *The 7 Habits of Highly Effective People* (New York: Simon and Schuster, 2004).

60   Reem Najjar, "Could new design standards enhance positive time-spent with technology?" UX Collective, March 27, 2020 (https://uxdesign.cc/could-new-design-standards-enhance-positive-time-spent-with-technology-8994541b58cf).

I'd never have achieved my goal of writing this book had I merely drifted through my days rather than taking decisive and intentional steps to eliminate capacity killers. Like the gasses we all learned about in high school chemistry, these activities will expand to fill the entire volume of your free time—if you let them.

2. *Crucial and time-constrained activities.* These are matters you must address immediately. If your house is on fire, all your other priorities fall away. You don't watch cat videos or engage in other capacity killers when the drapes are on fire. The same is true when your business or family faces a crisis. Sometimes these issues are simply unavoidable. But as we'll see in our third category, what we tend to dismiss as fate or bad luck often has its roots in actions we failed to take when time was still a luxury.

3. *Crucial but time-flexible activities.* This is the category in which ideally we should spend most of our time. If we are careful to block capacity killers from intruding into this more leisurely domain, we can take the kind of far-seeing and proactive measures that will stave off many of what later look like "inevitable" crises. Activities in this category include planning your second act S curve, thinking creatively (without your back to the wall), learning new skills, and building family relationships prior to an emergency.

Creating Capacity[61]

Capacity is about having time, energy, and money to fulfill your potential and create value for others. This margin enables us to explore a new direction for our lives and to have the resources to follow our inspired vision. Let's start with time. Where can you protect your time and create space in your calendar? In the grid on the next page, list the activities you regularly pursue in a typical week. Then answer the questions to the right of each activity.

---

61 This section adapts and repurposes materials from two sources: Strategic Coach (https://www.strategiccoach.com) and the Halftime Institute (https://halftimeinstitute.org).

Activity	Aligns with what Value/Goal?	Brings Joy? (Y/N)	Increase or Decrease?
1.			
2.			
3.			
4.			
5.			
6.			
7.			
8.			
9.			
10.			
Opportunities for Increasing Capacity			
List activities that are low-value and could be eliminated to create capacity.	1.		
	2.		
	3.		
	4.		
List high-value activities that could be combined or made more efficient.	1.		
	2.		
	3.		
	4.		

Figure 8.1 Creating Capacity

Be brutally honest about how you *actually* spend your time in a typical week rather than listing how you might *ideally* do so. Otherwise, you'll be unable to identify "Opportunities for Increasing Capacity" in the final part of the exercise.

The Importance of Saying No

Most of us say yes far too often. Hoping to please others, we nonchalantly take on commitments that can easily leave us with no margin to pursue our highest values, cultivate and apply our unique talents, or fend off the joyless feelings that inevitably come from being so overcommitted that we lose control of our lives. The following exercise will help you tame that reckless yes impulse in two ways:

1. By anticipating and rejecting entire categories of future "opportunities" that may tempt you with a momentary euphoria but eventually become—despite your best intentions—betrayals of what you most value. The point here is not just to avoid wasting time *doing* these activities but to avoid the opportunity costs of even *considering* them. Make a careful decision and stick to it. Don't resolve the same problem every week.

2. By eliminating any current obligations that do not align with what makes you come alive and—however innocuous they may seem—that keep the curtain from rising on your Act 2 calling.

The exercise draws on the distinction Nobel Prize–winning psychologist Daniel Kahneman makes between System 1 and System 2 thinking.[62] I'm simplifying a bit, but most of our decisions are made by System 1, which is easy, quick, and reflexive; although usually reliable, it's also prone to errors. System 2 thinking is slower, more deliberate, and more reliable. But we invoke it less often. System 1 is what offers that easy and automatic yes when we're asked to take on a new task. My aim here is to help you build in that momentary delay that allows System 2 to take over. And because this system calls up your deeper values, it offers a guilt-free way to politely decline offers that jeopardize those values.

---

62   Daniel Kahneman, *Thinking, Fast and Slow* (New York: Farrar, Straus, and Giroux, 2011).

Figure 8.2 Things to say no to.

Things to Say No To	Why?
1.	
2.	
3.	
4.	
5.	
6.	
7.	
8.	
Insights	
1.	
2.	
3.	

Wheat from Chaff

Being more discriminating about our use of "Yes!" doesn't mean the response to every new request should be "No!" Such a strategy is life-denying and an impediment to growth. But how do you sift the wheat of opportunities that are promising *for you* from the chaff of time-, energy-, and money-wasting distractions that *someone else* might find rewarding? I've found the following three-step heuristic particularly helpful in protecting my time and avoiding the regret that comes from either taking on a burdensome task or missing out on a genuine opportunity:

Begin by asking, "What will the new project or proposal accomplish if all goes well?" Be specific here. Make sure the result aligns with the values you expressed in chapter 6. Don't let your own goals get hijacked by someone else's enthusiasms, however noble or alluring they may be. Live your own Act 2, not someone else's.

Ask, "Are my gifts essential to this effort?" Causes that align with your values may not align with your skill set or with activities that bring you joy. Developing a vaccine for COVID-19 is valuable work, but unless you are a highly skilled biologist or someone with a passion for fundraising, what exactly do you bring to the table? How rewarding will you find your merely tangential role? And what will you give up by taking on such a role?

Ask, "What are the criteria for success? How will I measure progress? How will I know when I've accomplished my mission?" Unless you can identify achievable short-term goals and an ultimate end point, you're likely to find any new activity unrealistic and frustrating. Before you add anything to your to-do list, take the time to specify, in writing, how you intend to assess your efforts and what rewards you will feel at each stage of this progression. Unless you have satisfying and inspired answers here, you probably need to look for another Act 2 strategy.

Act 2: An Ideal Week

Most people spend more time planning for a weeklong vacation than they do for a thirty-five-year retirement. This worksheet is a simple planning tool to help you clarify how you'll spend an ideal week in Act 2. The goal here is to be intentional so that your week doesn't fill up with a series of haphazard and unrewarding events, what Ashley Whillans calls "time confetti."[63]

---

63 Ashley Whillans, *Time Smart: How to Reclaim Your Time and Live a Happier Life* (Cambridge, Massachusetts: Harvard Business Review Press, 2020).

Figure 8.3 The ideal week.

	Morning	Afternoon	Evening
Mon.			
Tues.			
Wed.			
Thurs.			
Fri.			
Sat.			
Sun.			

Renewable Energy

Having enough *time* to pursue your second act is only part of the challenge. You also need to safeguard and replenish your reserves of enthusiasm and energy. How can you do that?

Carve out days for spiritual renewal. I refer to these as "desert days"—though no desert is required. What's essential is that you periodically have some extended time alone for self-reflection. No electronics. No phones. No people. No to-do list. This is rarely an easy task, especially if you're a high achiever who's always striving to do and be better, but doing so can help you relax, recharge, and open your ears to guidance you may not even know you're seeking. Only by consciously shutting out the loud and habitual noise of your daily routines can you hear the subtler and more nuanced melodies that reconnect you to your larger purpose and sustain you through the difficult passages of your journey.

Only by consciously shutting out the loud and habitual noise of your daily routines can you hear the subtler and more nuanced melodies that reconnect you to your larger purpose and sustain you through the difficult passages of your journey.

Desert days give you the time you need to slow down and look at the big picture. Where do you want to be in twenty-five years? What relationships do you want to have fostered? What will bring the greatest meaning to your life? Lengthening your time horizon can help you slow down and focus on what really matters. I set aside a desert day each quarter. It's time well spent.

Take time off. This point is closely related to the previous one, but rather than spending time alone, focus on fun, hobbies, family, and friends. The key point is not to see this simply as a *reward* for doing hard work but as a *necessity* for enabling you to be creative in all areas of your life. When stuck on a physics problem, Albert Einstein would often put down his pen and pick up his violin. Time and again he found that the answer he'd been struggling to find appeared only when he took a break to relax and do something else.

Celebrate your wins. When you reach a milestone, pause and reflect on what you've accomplished. In the long run, you aren't delaying the full achievement of your goals. Instead, you're revitalizing yourself for the next stage in the process. I've found that a free app from the Strategic Coach called WinStreak˚ helps me feel positive about what I've accomplished at the end of each day and to clarify the wins I'll make on the next.[64]

Exercise regularly. The days of positing a duality between mind and body are long gone. The two are inextricably intertwined. A fulfilling second *act* requires *action*. You don't have to be a gym rat or workout fanatic, but you need to stay in shape to have the energy to enjoy those extra years we discussed in chapter 6. Two books I've found especially helpful are *Body for Life* by Bill Phillips and *Younger Next Year: A Guide to Living Like 50 Until You're 80 and Beyond* by Chris Crowley and Henry S. Lodge. Of course, a sensible diet and adequate sleep are essential to maximize the benefits of your exercise routine.

Go BIG! This is one of best pieces of advice I ever received. In this case "BIG" refers to "begin in gratitude." Researchers at Harvard University have shown that those who set aside a few minutes per day

---

64   I have no financial connection with the Strategic Coach company that produces this product. I'm merely endorsing a tool that has worked for me.

to reflect on what they are grateful for are happier than those who don't.[65] And that happiness helps maintain the energy margin we all need as we enter the second act of our lives.

Having clarified your *why* motivations, your unique talents, and your potential second act stages, having discussed the importance of developing and maintaining margins of time and energy, we'll now turn to the topic of wealth management and creating financial margin. Drawing on my thirty-six years of experience as a rationally optimistic financial advisor, I'll serve as your guide through the often confusing thickets of these and other topics:

- Evidence-based investing

- Goal-focused planning

- Retirement income planning

- Tax planning

- Risk management

- Estate planning

We'll also look at how psychological and biological factors can hinder wise investment decisions. The culmination of all that's come before, part 3 will provide the financial information to help you pursue the larger purposes we've identified in part 1 and part 2.

---

65   "Giving thanks can make you happier," June 17, 2020, *Harvard Health Publishing,* Harvard Medical School.

The Wealth Management Toolbox

CHAPTER 9

The Process

Process saves us from the poverty of our intentions.
—ELIZABETH KING[66]

Proven Approaches

I've opened this chapter with a quote from the American sculptor Elizabeth King because the sentiment applies as readily to wealth management—and a wide variety of other domains—as it does to artistic creation. In essence King is saying that success in any enterprise will elude us if we base our actions either on the unreliable day-by-day shifts in our moods and inspirations or on vague, grandiose (often delusional) visions with no clear benchmarks to tell us whether we're making progress, standing still, or heading for disaster.

What redeems our impoverished intentions is a clear and proven process that can withstand both our inevitable and all-too-human lapses in inspiration, as well as the distracting and generally erroneous

---

66 Elizabeth King, *Attention's Loop* (New York: Harry N. Abrams, 1999).

flights of fancy that threaten to pull us off course on a whim and scuttle all the steady progress we've made.

If your goal is to become a champion golfer, you need a process that will get you out of bed and off to the practice range when you'd rather sleep in—and also keep you from jumping on board to try out the latest fad exercise for adding thirty yards to your tee shot, ignoring its destructive impact on your lumbar vertebrae, and quickly converting you from a participant to a spectator.

In this chapter we'll focus on a proven process that eschews trendy too-good-to-be-true shortcuts, leads to success in wealth management, and protects us—literally and figuratively—from the poverty of even our best intentions. We'll pay special attention to the counterintuitive insight that we need to focus less on *outcomes* and more on *inputs*. Why? Because a shortsighted focus on the former can seduce us into following a deeply flawed process—for which we will suffer in the long run.

If your wealth management advisor bets all your money on the ball settling on red 21 from a single spin of a roulette wheel, and if luck is on your side, your outcome is undeniably positive. You'll cash in your chips and walk out of the casino financially transformed. But that doesn't mean your advisor's strategy was sound or that you'd be wise to double down on his advice for a second spin.

Crystal Balls and Butterfly Wings

Beware of advisors who claim to be able to predict the future of markets. Such "experts" are no more reliable than your daily horoscope or the stopped clock that's right twice per day. Instead, keep in mind the words of the economist Ezra Solomon: "The only function of economic forecasting is to make astrology look respectable."[67] Or as former Assistant Secretary of the Treasury Edgar Fiedler more bluntly put it, "He who lives by the crystal ball soon learns to eat ground glass."[68]

Clairvoyants make interesting characters in movies. In our unpredictable VUCA world (see chapter 5), however, they are invariably exposed as frauds. Mathematicians and physicists who study chaos theory speak of a phenomenon known as "the butterfly effect" in which tiny, unforeseen, impossible-to-calculate shifts in conditions (e.g., the flapping of a butterfly's wings in the Amazon) don't just slightly alter the precise predictive power of our most sophisticated models, but they also render them all but useless for detailed forecasts, particularly with respect to complex systems such as the economy. Only the foolish imagine that they can banish uncertainty from these realms. As students of quantum mechanics have proven, it's a fundamental property of the universe.[69]

Of course, that doesn't mean all financial outcomes are equally likely or that any attempt to plan for the future is misbegotten. But it does mean that we must learn to temper our expectations, find an astute and trustworthy guide, rely on a data-driven process that takes both probability and uncertainty into account, and remain true to that process during those momentary fluctuations that will inevitably occur in a universe in which disorder (or entropy) can be controlled but never banished.

---

67   Martin Wolf, "An Economist's Advice to Astrologers," *Financial Times*, January 6, 2015. This quote is often falsely attributed to John Kenneth Galbraith.

68   Barry Ritholtz, "Why Do Forecasters Keep Forecasting?" *The Big Picture*, December 11, 2013 (https://ritholtz.com/2013/12/why-do-forecasters-keep-forecasting/).

69   James Gleick, *Chaos: Making a New Science* (London: Minerva Press, 1996).

Rules, Habits, and Discipline

As an avid Georgia Bulldogs fan, it pains me to say this: under head coach Nick Saban, the University of Alabama's Crimson Tide has been the most successful college football program in the country. The key to Saban's unprecedented—and still growing—string of NCAA championships has been what he calls "the process."

Rather than concentrating on the result—a goal that, after all, is the same for every team and often depends on fortunate accidents—Saban systematically focuses on all the variables that are within his control: careful recruiting, year-round training, study habits that keep players eligible, blocking and tackling fundamentals, regimented practice sessions, teamwork, and eliminating distractions. In other words he cultivates the time-tested rules, habits, and discipline that give his team the best chance to win. His philosophy is that by attending to these matters, positive game-day outcomes will follow in a way that seldom happens when one simply recites clichés about "being the best." Everyone wants that. What separates Saban from his rivals are the specific steps he takes to turn the cliché into reality.[70]

Moving from the gridiron to the operating room, we again find that *process*—rather than inspired and unreliable moments of individual genius—generally pays the biggest dividends. The distinguished surgeon and author Atul Gawande developed an easily repeatable and systematic methodology—in the form of a nineteen-point checklist—for World Health Organization's Surgery Saves Lives Program. The result of implementing these clear protocols exceeded the author's

---

70   Nick Saban, *Nick Saban and the Process: Applying the Principles of the Greatest Football Coach in History to Your Life* (BroadBase Publishing@gmail.com: Lessons in Leadership Institute, 2018).

wildest expectations: across the eight hospitals that adopted the process, surgical deaths declined by 47 percent.[71]

Those preparing for their second act lives need a holistic wealth management guide who applies a Saban-like methodology to their finances. Rather than attempting to predict the future, your guide should take a structured and data-driven approach based on years of research. Avoid any guide who makes elaborate promises based on special forecasting skills. To recall a phrase

> *Rather than attempting to predict the future, your guide should take a structured and data-driven approach based on years of research.*

made popular by former Secretary of Defense Donald Rumsfeld, you're looking for someone who can *reduce* the number of "unknown unknowns" that might jeopardize your plans. Advisors who claim they can *eliminate* them are either deluded or lying. In either case they are not to be trusted.

And as the behavioral-scientist-turned-poker-champion Annie Duke points out, trusting your (or someone else's) gut or playing your hunches is a recipe for failure. Instead, we need to study the table and make our bets according to cold logic and probability, unclouded by adrenalized emotion or the rumblings of our digestive tract. Indeed, being rewarded for a foolish but lucky decision often encourages a dubious allegiance to high-risk, low-probability outcomes that over time will prove our undoing. "We don't win bets by being in love with our own ideas," Duke says. "We win bets by relentlessly striving to

---

71 Atul Gawande, *The Checklist Manifesto: How to Get Things Right* (New York: Picador, 2010).

calibrate our beliefs and predictions about the future to more accurately represent the world."[72]

The Financial Planning Process

All Certified Financial Planners must adhere to the following seven-step process specified by their regulatory board in its Code of Ethics and Standards of Professional Conduct.[73] As an informed consumer, you should expect the following from your Certified Financial Planner:

1. Understanding the client's personal and financial circumstances.

2. Identifying and selecting short- and long-term goals.

3. Analyzing the client's current course of action and potential alternative courses of action.

4. Developing one or more recommendations for maximizing the potential to meet the client's goals.

5. Presenting the recommendations to the client.

6. Implementing the financial planning recommendations.

7. Monitoring the process and updating the client's plan.

---

72   Annie Duke, *Thinking in Bets: Making Smarter Decisions When You Don't Have All the Facts* (New York: Portfolio, reprint edition 2019).

73   CFP Board's Code of Ethics and Standards of Professional Conduct (Practice Standards).

How to Find the Right Financial Advisor for Your Needs

Anyone new to working with a financial advisor might be surprised to find that the relationship will become quite personal. Unlike a simple business relationship, you'll want (and need) to share some of the most intimate aspects of your life. If your advisor is a good one, you'll spend as much time talking about the issues you hold close to your heart as you do about money.

That's why it's crucial to select an advisor to whom you can speak freely, someone you can trust with both your emotions and your money. So where do you begin? Here's a three-step guide to help find the right advisor for you:

STEP 1. UNDERSTAND HOW ADVISORY FEES WORK.

There are many types of advisors. One point that sets them apart is what they offer and how they are paid for their services.

Commission-based advisors. These include brokers, insurance agents, and registered representatives. Often employees of large financial services organizations, they sell financial products such as mutual funds, annuities, and insurance. Their menu of offerings is typically limited to what is offered by their employer, and like all salespeople, they receive commissions on the products they sell. This commission structure begs the question, whose best interest are they serving, yours or theirs?

Fee-only advisors. These independent advisors or firms are paid only by their clients to provide comprehensive financial advice and guidance. Their compensation is fully transparent and may include flat fees, hourly fees, a percentage of the assets under management

(AUM), or a combination of all three. Focused on each client's financial "big picture," they may offer a range of services, including estate planning, retirement planning, investments, tax planning (and sometimes preparation), insurance planning, and more. As fiduciaries, they are committed to serving in the best interest of their clients.

Fee-based advisors. A hybrid of sorts, these advisors are often affiliated with a broker-dealer. They may offer financial planning at an hourly rate, but like commission-based advisors, they may also hold a license to sell investments or insurance for a commission. That said, they do sell products, and they do receive commissions, so there remains a potential conflict of interest.

STEP 2. DECIDE WHAT KIND OF HELP YOU NEED.

Depending on your age, your level of assets, and the complexity of your finances, the kind of help you need will change throughout your lifetime. You'll want to be sure the advisor you choose can serve you today and far into your future.

Hourly consultations. If you need help with just one or two aspects of your financial life, such as buying a home, debt and cash flow management, selling a business, education funding, and so on, look for an advisor who offers project-based planning at an hourly rate. Some advisors will also offer a one-time financial plan designed to help you get organized and set goals—and to make recommendations—but don't offer ongoing consultations. Others do offer advice "as needed" at an hourly rate. This work is charged on a fee-only basis.

Comprehensive wealth management. As your money management needs become more complex, an advisor can help you plan all aspects of your finances to be sure everything is working together in pursuit of your goals. Covering everything from investing (asset management) and retirement planning to estate planning, insurance analysis, and more, the focus is long term and holistic. Services are generally charged on a fee-only basis, either a flat fee, a percentage of AUM, or both.

Pure asset management. If your focus is only on investing, an advisor can help you manage your assets over the long term. While managed separately from other areas of your financial life, the assets you accrue can help support your long-term financial goals. The cost for this work is generally an annual percentage of AUM.

STEP 3. APPLY YOUR SELECTION CRITERIA.

Once you've determined what services you need and how you want to pay, evaluate prospects according to the following criteria:

Education and experience. Consider how long the advisor has been in practice and other experience (e.g., being a business owner or working in a corporate environment). Credentials are not merely decorative: they indicate training in specific areas of financial planning. An advisor with professional designations such as Certified Financial Planner', Certified Fund Specialist, Accredited Investment Fiduciary, Chartered Financial Consultant, or Chartered Financial Analyst has completed extensive coursework and training in these areas. And as we've seen, some designations, such as the CFP, require adherence to strict ethical standards as well as ongoing education.

Ethics. Before entrusting someone with your hard-earned money, be sure they are ethical. FINRA—the Financial Industry Regulatory Authority—requires all advisors to be listed on BrokerCheck.[74] This online listing tells you if an advisor is legally registered to provide investment advice and what products they are able to sell (stocks, bonds, mutual funds, etc.). BrokerCheck also gives you a snapshot of

---

74   Visit https://brokercheck.finra.org.

your potential advisors' employment history, licensing information, and any regulatory actions, arbitrations, or complaints against them.

Relational fit. No matter how perfect an advisor's background, skills, and ethics may be, it's important to trust your gut when it comes to your personal fit. Ask yourself the following five questions:

1. Is this someone I want to be in a close relationship with for the next twenty to thirty years?

2. Do they seem open and honest?

3. Can I communicate easily with them?

4. Do they work with people like me—with my needs and level of assets—and who think the way I do?

5. Can this advisor create enough value (both tangible and emotional) for the fees they charge?

If you answer no to any of these questions, keep looking. If you answered them all with an enthusiastic "Yes!" trust your (well-informed) gut: You've found the right advisor for you.

What to Expect: A Case Study

Thus far in this chapter, I've been speaking mostly in the abstract, offering a kind of skeleton outline of the financial planning process. In this final section, I'd like to put some meat on those bones and give you a clearer sense of what to expect (and demand) in the way of process, planning, and precision. To that end I'll walk you through the four-step process we've established at my company, TandemGrowth Financial Advisors.[75]

Figure 9.1 The TandemGrowth process.

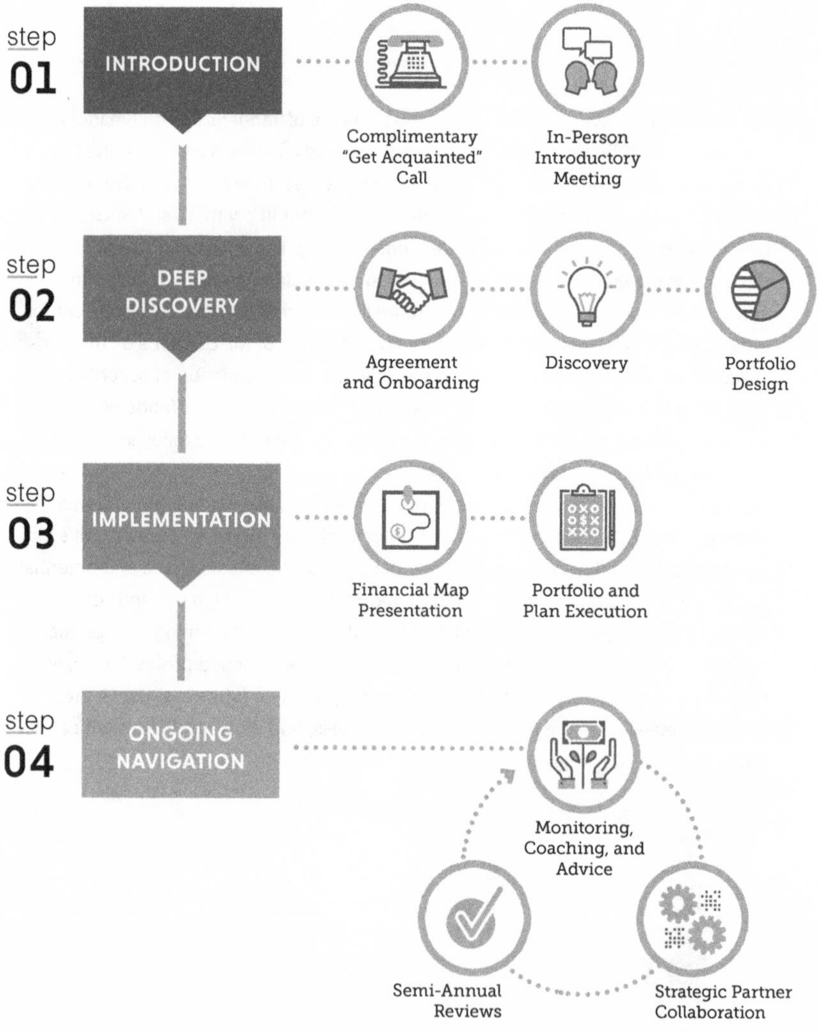

STEP 1. INTRODUCTION

This consists of two parts: the first is a complimentary get-acquainted call to ascertain whether we believe our company's approach is a good fit for the client or whether their goals and objectives might be better met by another provider. Readers should understand that—just as the title "pilot" can refer to a skilled practitioner in the cockpit of a helicopter, a commercial airline's Boeing 747, or an Air Force F-22 Raptor—the common title "financial advisor" encompasses a broad and divergent range of operating strategies.

It's a big tent.

In chapter 14, I'll discuss my evidence-based investment philosophy, but for now it's enough to know that—when it comes to general wealth management—the underlying philosophy of a financial advisor will vary widely from firm to firm. So I find that it's crucial to begin by ensuring that you're working from the same playbook. And here's one of the critical differentiators readers should look for:

- Those who take the *goal-focused* and *planning-driven* approach I advocate.

- Those who apply a *market-focused* and *performance-driven* strategy—and thus focus primarily on outcomes.

As I've made clear above, I'm in the camp that maintains that you can't control outcomes and that the best course is to follow a proven process.

So the introductory phone call is informal and takes about twenty minutes. And I ask the prospective client for basic information: Tell me about yourself and your family. Tell me why you're looking for an advisor. What would you consider an ideal advisory relationship? Are you looking for a holistic coaching process?

If we seem to be well aligned, I'll set up the second part of the introduction process: an in-person (or a virtual) meeting to confirm that initial impression and get a clearer picture of the client's personal and financial circumstances. Keep in mind that this is a mutual selection process, for which I believe there are three important factors in establishing a good fit. First, do we have the services to meet the client's needs? Second, do we feel comfortable together on a personal level? I always say I can't teach anyone to be a wealth manager in the four to eight hours I get to spend with them a year. So you've got to have open, honest communication and a trusting relationship. And if your gut tells you that we're not the firm for you, you should honor that instinct. And the final factor is economic: Can we create enough value for you for the fees that we charge? If we can't do that, it would be irrational for you to hire us. And we wouldn't want you to.

The "Tandem" in my company name isn't just rhetorical. We want to ensure we can work together in ways that are *mutually* beneficial. And part of what makes us unique is that we start with meaning and purpose. Even in that first meeting, I begin with "What is your *why*?" And then I ask them the three George Kinder questions that we discussed in chapter 6.

Now some people will balk at this point and say, "Look, I don't really want my advisor to ask me those kinds of personal questions. I don't want to go that deep. I want someone to build me a portfolio and focus on the money." That's fine. But such reluctance doesn't allow us to do what we are trained and motivated to do, and those clients will be better served by another kind of advisor.

STEP 2. DEEP DISCOVERY

This step begins with onboarding. Following best practices, we provide you with a document that clearly outlines what we're doing, what our responsibilities are, what your responsibilities are, what you're being charged, the terms under which you can fire us if we're not meeting your expectations, and so on. Next, we collect all the data we need to do our job—getting tax returns, employee-benefits booklets, and estate planning documents as well as connecting all of your accounts to our systems so we can monitor and build an accurate balance sheet and prepare an asset allocation analysis.

After that, you come in for a collaborative discovery meeting at which we get down to the real work—clarifying your financial history; discussing your hopes, dreams, and fears; and starting to construct a portfolio designed to take you from where you are now to where you want to be in your ideal future. We spend enough time with you to clarify how much risk we believe you *need to take*, how much risk you're *willing to take*, and how much risk you *have the capacity to take*. We also educate you on how the capital markets work and on our process-oriented philosophy.

In order to build detailed and custom financial plans, we usually begin by asking questions to uncover the *ideal plan*. This is the pie-in-the-sky scenario if everything in your life and the capital markets go perfectly—the plan that offers you the highest level of spending, giving, legacy, and education costs as well as your earliest retirement date and the lowest number of financial risks.

But because, in a VUCA world, few strategies work out ideally, we also ask detailed questions to determine a *minimum plan*. In other words what is the longest you could see yourself working; what is the least amount of spending, legacy, gifts, and so on you'd settle for; and what is the most financial risk you're able or willing to take? Do you want to work longer, or do you want to retire at the same time with less income? Do you want to retire at the same time but accept more market uncertainty, or do you want to take less market uncertainty and retire later? Thus we set upper and lower parameters at the start of the plan-design process so we can build plans A, B, C, and D. By deciding in advance what trade-offs you'd be willing to make in the event of personal or global difficulties, we're ready for the many possibilities the world may throw at you. Of course, as circumstances and goals evolve, we work with you to tweak these plans at every stage of your journey.

STEP 3. IMPLEMENTATION

Next, we present the financial map. Based on our analysis after step 2, we'll provide you with multiple scenarios and explain various trade-offs. This is an iterative process. We're homing in on the target based on your feedback as you continue to clarify and refine your goals. I always emphasize that we *collaborate*; we don't *dictate*.

Once we settle on the plan together, we move on to portfolio and plan execution. As we've discussed in earlier chapters, a great plan doesn't have any value in the abstract. You have to implement it.

> *A great plan doesn't have any value in the abstract. You have to implement it.*

That could involve updating your will, paying off your house, rebalancing your portfolio, and aligning your investments. We'll explore these issues more fully in later chapters.

We're not the only people involved in the implementation process. We help our clients by collaborating with CPAs, attorneys, bankers, insurance experts in long-term care, tax advisors, Medicare supplement specialists. We're still directing the second act, but we're going to call in experts we trust to design the sets, provide the lighting, sell tickets, and so on.

STEP 4. ONGOING NAVIGATION

We're not being paid just to create a plan. We're being paid to adjust the plan as life's contingencies impinge on it: maybe you lose a job, suffer a serious illness, win the lottery. Whatever occurs, for good or bad, we want to be one of the first people you call for advice. It's this ongoing coaching we're most passionate about. Our hope is that by offering wisdom and access, we're providing clients with the clarity and confidence to live a great life.

One way we seek to do that is by setting up a review meeting every six months. Although our clients know that we are available as needed, this process helps keep us on track and provides our clients with a nudge to remind them, "Here's what you said you wanted to do, here's why you wanted to do it, and here are the things you haven't done yet." So these meetings impose some vital discipline on both the client and us to meet our commitments.

But in addition to the semi-annual reviews, we're monitoring your plan in real time. We don't just gather that information twice a year for the sake of the meeting. If you're overfunded or underfunded, we'll both know it because we provide you with a client portal so we can monitor your progress together. As needed, we'll come back to you with new advice throughout the year.

In the next chapter, we'll explore the essential—but often over-looked—topic of risk management.

CHAPTER 10

Risk Management

We insure against what can go wrong in order to acquire
the luxury of investing for what can go right.
—NICK MURRAY[76]

The Risks of Ignoring Risk

Because this chapter is about managing risk, I'll start with a cautionary note. As you build your Act 2 wealth management plan and as you evaluate guides for your journey, be aware that many advisors focus solely on managing investments and ignore the holistic approach I'm advocating. So if you're looking for a holistic plan, cast a cold eye on any guide who fails to address risk management.

Such guides generally avoid this topic for two reasons. First, managing investments can be scalable and profitable to advisory firms, which means they may have an incentive to devote a disproportionate amount of time to such matters—and thus downplay risk. Second,

---

76 Nick Murray, *Simple Wealth, Inevitable Wealth* (Southold, New York: The Nick Murray Company, 2004).

discussing potential setbacks is inherently less exciting than talking about financial growth. No one is especially keen to plan for the possibility of getting disabled, dying prematurely, or having a lengthy stay in a hospital, but we all love to talk about investments, the capital markets, and becoming the next Warren Buffett.

Risk management is about keeping what you have and providing security for yourself and those you care about.

Nonetheless, financial advisors do a terrible disservice to their clients if they don't address things that can go wrong. Risk management is about keeping what you have and providing security for yourself and those you care about. Do you really want to ignore difficult topics and jeopardize yourself and your loved ones because it's more pleasant to talk as if your life will always run as smoothly as a rising escalator? A responsible financial plan must address things that could go wrong because, in a VUCA world, some of them certainly will. That's why risk management is at the foundation of the financial planning pyramid. Without that solid base, your second act is in constant—and unnecessary—jeopardy.

Long-Term Wealth
Accumulation Capital

Emergency Reserve Capital

Risk Management

Figure 10.1 The financial planning pyramid.

Most of us tend to downplay risk, but we do so at our peril. You probably don't expect to become injured and unable to work—and to lose your income. Nonetheless, data from the Social Security Administration shows that this fate awaits one of every four working adults.[77] Are you comfortable accepting a 25 percent risk that, without disability insurance, you'll be unable to provide for your family? Do you really want to work with an advisor who fails to address these important issues?

Managing risk requires both diligence and the thorough process we discussed in the previous chapter. A reliable guide must prompt you to have difficult conversations about your family needs in the event of death, a disabling illness, litigation, or property loss. Any discomfort you feel during the conversation will pale in comparison with what you'll endure when (not *if*) you face one of these issues without adequate preparation. Indeed, studies show that, for some, being out of work for one year can wipe out ten years of savings.[78]

I could write an entire book about risk management. In this chapter, however, we'll focus on the big-picture elements and explore the importance of preparing for the unexpected. My aim is to provide a broad overview (i.e., not a comprehensive analysis).

Health Insurance

A 2019 study by the *American Journal of Public Health* found that 66.5 percent of all US bankruptcies resulted from medical expenses

---

77   "Disability Benefits," Social Security Administration, accessed May 3, 2022, https://www.ssa.gov/pubs/EN-05-10029.pdf.

78   Jeff Bernier, "Why Risk Management Should Be Part of a Holistic Wealth Management Plan," *Money and Meaning* podcast, September 15, 2020.

or the loss of income due to illness or injury.[79] People who require a monthlong stay in the hospital can easily run up a bill in excess of $500,000, thus wiping out both their savings and retirement accounts. With the stakes that high, health insurance isn't optional. You can't afford to be without it.

There are three basic types of coverage: individual, group/employer, and Medicare.

Obviously most people who are working have group coverage, which offers some tax benefits to the employer and potential tax benefits to the employee. We'll discuss these issues more fully in chapter 11. Employees typically have two or three different plans from which to choose. So part of the job of your financial advisor is to help you select the coverage that best fits your unique circumstances.

These plans all have deductibles you pay up front, which is a way for you to have some skin in the game and discourage frivolous use. There's also coinsurance, which requires both you and the insurance company to pay a portion of the cost. Finally, there's usually a cap, your maximum out-of-pocket expense. Every plan has networks that enable you to get higher levels of coverage, but virtually all of them set an upper limit on the amount you'll have to pay. That figure should be one of your chief considerations.

Any attempt to cover the full range of complexities related to your Medicare decisions would more than double the length of this book. Indeed, the "simple" enrollment booklet you'll receive when you are sixty-four is 120 pages long. And it's not a page-turner! Because the "ideal" choice depends on conditions unique to your own circumstances (e.g., Are you still working and covered by your employer's

---

79   David U. Himmelstein, Robert M. Lawless, Deborah Thorne, Pamela Foohey, and Steffie Woolhandler, "Medical Bankruptcy: Still Common Despite the Affordable Care Act," *AJPH*, March 2019.

insurance?) and because a failure to choose wisely and apply at the appropriate time can expose you to catastrophic risks, you must begin planning well in advance of your sixty-fifth birthday, preferably with a financial advisor who works (as my firm does) with experts trained in the ever-changing nuances of Medicare regulations. This is clearly an area where collaboration with a Medicare expert is critical.

Medicare Part A helps pay for inpatient care in a hospital or for a limited time at a nursing facility (following a hospital stay). Part A also pays for some home healthcare and hospice care. Medicare Part B (medical insurance) helps pay for services from doctors and other healthcare providers, outpatient care, home healthcare, medical equipment, and some preventive services. Your Part A benefits are free. Your Part B benefits are not. Costs are based on your income. We'll discuss the specifics more fully in the next chapter when we talk about tax planning. You can also consult the table at the Social Security Administration's website under the heading "Premiums: Rules For Higher-Income Beneficiaries."[80]

Because there are limits to what Part B will cover, almost everyone should purchase either a Medicare Advantage Plan (Part C) or a Medicare Supplement Plan (Medigap). Finally, Part D is a prescription drug card, which you'll typically get from a private company. Finding the right plans to support your Part B coverage is enormously complex, and few applicants are likely to make an optimal choice without professional help.

Timing is crucial. Unless you are still working and covered by another plan, you have to enroll for Parts A and B during a seven-month window that includes the month you turn sixty-five and the

---

80   "Premiums: Rules for Higher-Income Beneficiaries," Social Security Administration, accessed May 3, 2022, https://www.ssa.gov/benefits/medicare/medicare-premiums.html.

three months before or after.[81] You'll pay a steep penalty if you don't enroll on time. If you retire past age sixty-five, you have an eight-month special enrollment period from the date your employment ends or the date your employer's insurance coverage stops (whichever comes first).

None of this is especially exciting, but any responsible wealth management plan has to budget for these expenses. And "excitement" is precisely what you don't want with your Medicare plan. I tell my clients, "Look, you may be paying $1,000 a month for your part B premium and your supplement and your drug cards. But when you go to the doctor, you'll be paying very little, and if you have a catastrophic event, your out-of-pocket expenses are really limited. You're much better off paying a fixed cost in retirement and avoiding the horrific prospect of facing a $500,000 bill that will bankrupt you."

To see just one head-spinning and counterintuitive example of a pitfall you can unwittingly stumble into without professional guidance, consider someone who has been working past sixty-five and opts for an employer-offered COBRA insurance policy after being laid off. From her point of view, everything looks and feels the same about her employer coverage. But as soon as the tie between work and insurance is severed, she enters a new category. Unless she enrolls in Medicare Parts A and B, she no longer has a primary payer. The COBRA policy she was counting on has become her secondary payer. If she ends up in an emergency room, she will be on the hook for 80 to 90 percent of the bill.[82]

---

81 If your birthday is on the first of the month, your window is four months before and two months after your birth month.

82 For more information on Medicare complexities, listen to my conversation with Melinda Caughill on the June 16, 2020, *Money and Meaning* podcast.

Disability Insurance

Also known as "income replacement insurance," a disability plan can be more important than life insurance for many people. Why? Because if you are middle-aged or younger, your future earnings are likely your biggest asset. Many people insure their lives, but according to *Forbes*, at any point in your working career, you are more likely to become disabled than to die.[83] What safety net do you have if—like one in four Americans—you experience a lengthy period when you can't work?

Health insurance coverage will never replace the income you lose while you are unable to work. As Colin Nabity notes, "Workers' compensation only applies to accidents on the job. If you're lucky, paid sick leave and your emergency fund savings will be able to provide some relief, but likely not for long. Individual long-term disability insurance can keep you afloat financially for the length of the benefit period on your policy (anywhere from two years up until retirement)."

I usually present my clients with the following example: Without disability insurance, if you're making $100,000 a year, you're earning $8,333 a month. And if you become disabled, you get nothing. And, as Nabity points out, "70 percent of working Americans would experience financial hardship within a month of losing their paycheck." On the other hand, if you have a disability policy that costs you $3,000 a year, you're still earning $8,083 per month (after paying the premium) while you're working, but if you become disabled, you'll receive $5,500 a month potentially tax-free. So you're trading $300 a month to guarantee roughly 66 percent of your pre-disability income.

---

83   Colin Nabity, "Four Reasons Disability Insurance Might Belong In Your Financial Plan," Forbes Finance Council, May 27, 2020.

There are two types of disability plans: group and individual. Group insurance provides significant coverage at a low cost, and it's where many people should start. Plans you pay for individually are more expensive but offer much better terms. Unlike group plans, they are generally portable. They are also much more flexible in how they define "disability," allowing you to tailor the terms to your own occupation. So for example, if you're a surgeon or a pianist and you damage your hand, you'll be covered in a way that someone who doesn't require such fine motor skills might not be.

With individual plans you generally want a "noncancelable and guaranteed renewable contract." That means the insurance company can't change the price or the provisions. One final detail to keep in mind: If you have a policy *your employer pays for*, the benefits will be taxable; if it's a policy *you pay for*, the benefits will be *tax-free*.

Long-Term Care Insurance

Many years ago long-term care insurance got a bad name because companies used aggressive sales tactics to sell policies to seniors who were not well-informed. In the last fifteen or twenty years, the government and the companies have cleaned up the industry and created some viable products that can help if you become unable to take care of yourself, unable to perform what are called "activities of daily living": bathing, eating, going to the bathroom, and so on. This insurance is designed to reimburse you for the costs or to provide income so you can pay them yourself. In many of these contracts, you can be cared for at home or in a nursing facility.

Who needs to consider this kind of insurance? People with low income or assets typically can't afford it. They often think Medicare will cover long-term care costs, but that's not true. In some cases

Medicaid may be an option. At the other end of the spectrum, affluent people may not need it because they can self-insure; they have enough assets or income to pay for this care without transferring the risk to an insurance company.

So the people most interested in this coverage will be what I call the "big middle": those with a household worth below $5 million. For them, shifting the risk to an insurance company may be a wise decision. They'll have two basic options.

The first is traditional long-term care insurance, which is kind of like homeowner's insurance, meaning you pay a premium. And if you never file a claim, your premium dollars just went out the door. Just as when you buy homeowner's insurance, if your house doesn't burn down, you don't get anything for it. You just insured that risk. Many years ago I was of the opinion that this was the best type of coverage for most people. Basically it's just term insurance. You're paying a monthly or an annual premium, and if you need long-term care, this coverage pays you a daily benefit.

The second option is what I call *hybrid products*, which combine long-term care benefits with life insurance. Until about ten years ago, I was not a big fan. The products seemed too complex and expensive. But over the past decade, these products have improved significantly, and I now think they can play an important role for people who want—or need—to combine their life insurance coverage with their long-term care coverage. And essentially that's how these products work: they're life insurance contracts modified to provide a prepayment of the death benefit if you need long-term care.

Life Insurance and Survivor Needs

People need life insurance for three broad reasons. The first and most important is to replace income. If you have a spouse and children, and you're the breadwinner, you want to protect the people that you care about in the event you die prematurely. This is most important early in your career when you are still building wealth. But I tell my clients that their ultimate goal should be to build enough wealth so that they are self-insured with their own assets, and thus they may no longer need life insurance to provide for their survivors.

I tell my clients that their ultimate goal should be to build enough wealth so that they are self-insured with their own assets, and thus they may no longer need life insurance to provide for their survivors.

The graph below illustrates my point. If we look at line AB, we see that the amount of money your survivors need goes down every day that you live. This is simple arithmetic. If you die when your spouse is fifty, they will need less support than if you'd died when they were twenty. So the amount you need for survivor income declines steadily throughout your life.

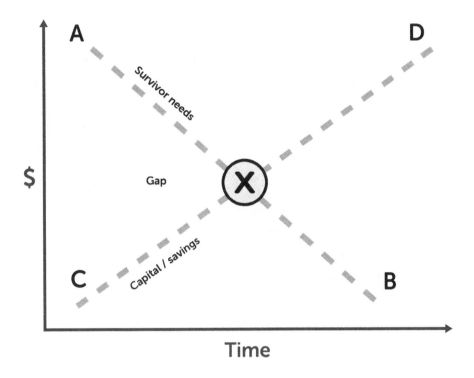

Figure 10.2 Survivor income "gap" declines as your wealth grows.

Now if we look at the upward-sloping line CD, we see that, in all likelihood, your wealth will increase every year you work. And where the lines intersect, we see an X. The space between line XA and XC is the steadily shrinking gap between your survivor needs and your wealth. Life insurance is designed to close that gap. And at point X, you are self-insured with your assets and no longer need life insurance to provide for your survivors—though as we will see later, you may want it for other reasons.

How do you determine your survivors' needs? By working with your financial advisor to complete a "capital needs analysis." In essence you're answering this question: if I should die prematurely without accumulating the necessary assets, what do I want to provide for my survivors? This could include income to a spouse, support for your children, money for college, and mortgage payments.

Then you do a present value calculation to say "Okay, if I died today, how much capital would it require to fund those goals?" And you back out your existing resources so assets that you already have would come off that, and you buy a policy that will meet the needs you've enumerated.

The second reason for having life insurance is to provide cash if you have a collection of *illiquid* assets (i.e., they can't readily be converted to cash). So if you're a business owner, for example, and all of your wealth is tied up in your company, life insurance can be really helpful to provide liquidity so your heirs can continue to run your business rather than having to sell it at an unfavorable, fire-sale rate to get quick cash. The same is true for someone with significant real estate assets.

The third reason is that life insurance offers a tax-efficient way to make a leveraged gift. So if I want to leave a million dollars to the University of Georgia or to my church, but I don't have a million dollars sitting around to give them—and I don't want to disinherit my kids—I can pay a life insurance premium of, say, $5,000 every year with the university or my church as the beneficiary. And at my death, they'll receive $1 million.

There are two general types of life insurance: term or permanent, but which type you purchase matters less than getting the amount of coverage determined by your capital needs analysis. People often buy permanent policies because they've been convinced that life insurance is a good investment. I don't agree with this strategy, but leaving that aside for now, I'm particularly opposed to focusing so intensely on the policy's investment features that buyers fail to secure sufficient funds to cover their survivors' needs. The quality of the carrier matters a great deal as well. Keep in mind that these companies are making a long-term promise to you. We need them to be around so they can fulfill that promise.

With term insurance, you're paying a small premium over a fixed number of years. It's ideal for a young couple who need a lot of coverage and expect to be saving money and building wealth over time. It's probably the most efficient approach for most people, providing the maximum coverage for the least amount of outlay. If you get a ten-year term or longer, I recommend buying a contract that gives you the option of converting it to permanent contract.

With permanent insurance, you have two options: *traditional whole life* and *universal life*. If the goal is estate liquidity or to make a leveraged gift, these can be more effective than term insurance. But they are a lot more expensive. They also have a cash value element, so one portion of your premium pays for the death benefit year to year, and another portion is going into a cash value.

With a traditional whole life policy, you're basically a shareholder in the insurance company. Although not especially flexible, these policies can still be great products. Universal life combines term and permanent: you know the premium you're paying for the term element, and you know how much is going into the cash value fund. These polices can be flexible, but depending on the type of contract, the guarantees could be weaker, although this has changed for the better in recent years.

As we enter the second act of our lives, many of us are self-insured, so we don't need as much life insurance as we once did. But you may find yourself with a lot of these old permanent policies. That's when a policy audit can be extremely valuable. If you have some old universal or whole life policy that has cash value that you no longer need for survivor needs or to make a leveraged gift, why not exchange it, if you're in reasonably good health, to one of these hybrid long-term care products and use that cash value to make the purchase? Basically you're taking this life insurance that you no longer need and converting it to solve your long-term care need.

You could also use these old policies to make leveraged gifts. So for instance, you can say, "I have this universal or whole life policy that's paid up, but I don't need it anymore. What do I do with it?" Your financial advisor can help you get creative here. You could change the beneficiary to a charity. Or, even better, you could change the beneficiary of one of your IRAs to a charity and use this life insurance for the heir that's not getting the IRA. So you've given your heir a tax-free death benefit, and you've given the charity a traditional IRA that would have been all taxable to your heir. Or if these contracts have reasonably good internal rates of return on the cash value, you could keep them as part of your emergency reserve capital.

Property and Casualty Insurance / Asset Protection

This insurance protects you if your house burns down, if you total your car, or, since we live in a litigious society, if you get sued. If you're on the board of a company, you might need directors and officers insurance. Anyone who has accumulated substantial capital should have additional coverage, an umbrella liability policy that fits on top of the liability limits of your automobile and home insurance. The key here is to have a qualified agent do an audit every two or three years to protect the assets you've accumulated.

If you own businesses, obviously you need comprehensive commercial lines property and liability insurance. If you own rental real estate, you probably want to speak with a lawyer about owning those properties in separate LLCs to provide another layer of protection. If you're in a job that comes under a lot of scrutiny (e.g., an anesthesiologist), you might want to put a moat around your other assets so that a frivolous lawsuit does not put you at risk.

In the next chapter, we'll review a variety of issues related to tax planning.

CHAPTER 11

Tax Planning

*For my tax evasion, I should be punished. For my
tax avoidance, I should be commended.*
—SUPREME COURT JUSTICE LOUIS BRANDEIS[84]

Free Bridges

In the quote above, Judge Brandeis is referring to his daily commute: when in a hurry, he crossed the Potomac on a toll bridge and paid for the convenience; most days, however, he took a slightly longer drive outside the downtown area to another bridge, which the city erected to limit traffic snarls. How? Through a financial incentive: those willing to make the detour could cross for free.

Brandeis says that if he used the toll bridge without paying, he would be guilty of tax evasion. But if he crosses the free bridge, he is "using a legitimate, logical and suitable method of tax avoidance, and am performing a useful social service by doing so." He concludes,

---

84   Joshua Schlinsky, "How Will Future Taxes Affect Your Money?" *Forbes*, May 30, 2019.

"The tragedy of life today is that so few people know that the free bridge even exists."

I've introduced tax planning in the wealth management toolbox not as a "tax expert" but as a practitioner in the trenches for thirty-six years. I put theory into practice and help clients find the free bridges they're entitled to use, not so they can shirk their civic duty, but so they can fulfill it in the ways they find most meaningful. Don't misunderstand me: I believe we must all pay our fair share to cover government services. But I also believe we have the right, and even the responsibility, to exert some control over how that money is used.

Let me explain: All of our financial resources are either *social* or *personal* capital. The former is that part of our wealth we must contribute to society, either through taxes or charitable gifts. We don't get to keep our social capital. I view tax planning as a way to direct more of that money to institutions that share our values and less to bureaucratic institutions that do not. In other words I see it as a more mindful way to fulfill our social obligation—and as another way to align our means with our life's meaning.

I write frequently about the futility of trying to forecast the investment markets. Attempting to predict what a future congress or president will do with tax legislation is equally futile. Following Judge Brandeis, my goal is to take the current tax laws, look at your future prospects, and use the "free bridges" where appropriate. Doing so frees up more capital for you to give or enjoy. It can also reduce the volatility in your investment portfolios. If you can save a significant amount each year in taxes, the return required to meet your goals could be lower, and you could therefore reduce the level of risk you're exposed to in the capital markets.

Integrated Tax Planning

Before we get into specific tax planning strategies, keep in mind that all these decisions should be carefully integrated into your overall wealth management plan. Modular or piecemeal planning almost always proves ineffective because you end up trying to achieve separate goals that at best are not in sync and at worst are in open conflict. Your tax and investment strategies, Social Security claiming choices, estate planning strategies—none of these can be optimized individually because they all affect each other.

Just as a basketball coach can't choose five players without considering how they will work together as a team and how their individual skills will complement each other, so you can't choose an efficient tax plan unless it harmonizes with all the other components of your overarching financial plan. Otherwise, the pieces can easily negate each other by working at cross purposes. Unless you plan holistically, you'll be like a chef who blends two incompatible recipes—either of which might have been fine—and ends up putting chocolate frosting on a salmon fillet.

Tax Location Strategy

When we hear "Location! Location! Location!" most of us think of real estate decisions. But where you "locate" your investments (i.e., the types of accounts you choose) can have an enormous impact on your tax bill. Just as you diversify your investments, so you'll want to diversify your tax strategies. Ideally

> *Where you "locate" your investments (i.e., the types of accounts you choose) can have an enormous impact on your tax bill. Just as you diversify your investments, so you'll want to diversify your tax strategies.*

that means you'll want to own three types of vehicles: taxable, tax-free, and tax-deferred.

Essentially asset location planning is about trying to pack the tax-free or tax-deferred accounts with recommended asset classes that are the *least tax efficient* so that you minimize your exposure in those areas with the worst tax implications. If you have assets that generate high levels of ordinary income, we would generally like to own those inside tax-sheltered accounts (e.g., traditional or Roth IRAs).

Conversely we want to stuff the taxable accounts with *the most tax efficient asset classes*, such as large cap US equities, where you receive less expensive capital gains treatment compared with ordinary income, which is taxed at higher rates. If you've owned one of these assets for at least a year, taxes on gains are generally capped at a 15 percent capital gains rate. Moreover, if these assets prove more volatile, you can harvest the losses in taxable accounts.

In a diversified portfolio, you'll have exposure to cash, bonds, stocks, real estate, and emerging markets. If you own taxable bonds where most of the return comes from interest, not appreciation, and that interest is taxed every year at ordinary income rates, you'd like to own these inside the sheltered account. The same is true with higher-yielding real estate securities.

My purpose here is not to run through all the minutiae about tax location strategies. The two key takeaways are that the location of your investments will substantially affect your tax bill and that the layperson is likely to overlook a lot of the free bridges without the help of a guide. Remember, what you keep is far more important than what you earn.

To work most effectively with a financial advisor, you'll want to know both your average and marginal tax rates. The first refers to the total amount of tax you pay divided by your income (i.e., your total tax burden). The second is the rate you pay on the next dollar you earn (i.e., your highest tax rate). You should also know your adjusted gross income (AGI). This is the total amount you earned in a year (your gross income) minus certain deductions or "adjustments." Although your gross income is the starting point for determining your total tax liability, many tax preferences and phaseouts are based on your AGI. All of this can easily be obtained from your last year's tax return. Finally, you should know how much you have in taxable, tax-free, and tax-deferred accounts. With this information, you and your advisor can start making wiser tax decisions.

Spending Strategy

As you move into your life's second act, you'll likely be relying more on your capital, pensions, and Social Security than on a monthly paycheck. How you distribute that wealth can have a huge impact on your tax liability, so it's important to recognize that the strategies that we use to *distribute* wealth could differ somewhat from the strategies we used to *accumulate* it.

I've found that what we call *The TandemGrowth Retirement Distribution System* works extremely well in large part because it produces both psychological and financial benefits. And the psychological benefits are more important than most people realize because they encourage you to stick with the plan. I'm not sure a theoretically perfect plan exists, but as a thought experiment, let's say that it does. If that hypothetical plan is too complex or stressful, you're likely to abandon it.

While academic evidence can show that this retirement distribution system may not be necessary and that simply taking systematic distributions from a diversified portfolio can produce similar results, we still recommend that our clients consider it. Why? Because it produces great results, provides a sense of security, and is a model you're likely to adhere to for the long haul. That last point is crucial: a so-called "perfect" plan becomes worthless if you abandon it. Think of all the "perfect" diets and workouts that people give up on after about two weeks. Choosing a reliable plan that you can commit to both logically and emotionally will, in large part, determine its worth.

Three Buckets

The foundational metaphor for this plan is to think of your money in three buckets. The first is our emergency reserve capital. Dave Ramsey calls this "Murphy repellent." It's protection against the law that whatever can go wrong eventually will go wrong. I advise my clients to keep three to six months' worth of expenses in this bucket. The money sits at a bank, earning no real return (after inflation), but it's safe and liquid; it's there when your roof leaks, your car engine goes on the fritz, or a child has an emergency. So if your monthly expenses are $10,000 a month, we'd want you to keep $30,000 to $60,000 sitting in an FDIC-insured account somewhere.

The second bucket is your short-term portfolio, generally two years' worth of anticipated distributions from your capital. So for instance, if you need $15,000 a month to cover all your expenses, and you have $5,000 a month coming in from pensions and Social Security, you'd need $10,000 a month from your investment capital. That amounts to $240,000 for two years. From this account, our client would be getting a $10,000 direct deposit to their checking account. These accounts are placed in low-volatility, low-expected return investments. In the past we would use a combination of short-term fixed-income securities and Treasury money market funds. At the time of this writing, our desire to protect against interest rate risks has us recommending Treasury money market funds and FDIC-insured accounts only for the short-term portfolio.

The reason it's psychologically comfortable is that at the first of every year, our clients know they have two years' worth of spending that's not in the more volatile long-term portfolio. And this money can be very tax efficient because we would, ideally, fund the short-term portfolio with taxable accounts (not IRAs or annuities). The money you're distributing from that account is tax-free because you're doing something that your grandparents, who were children of the Depression, warned you about: "Never eat the principal! Whatever you do, live off the income." And we're eating the principal in this short-term portfolio account.

Now to make you and your grandparents feel better, you're not eating the principal when you look at the entirety of your financial assets. But you are definitely doing so in this one account. That's what makes it tax efficient: you're spending the principal in this one account and not taking taxable distributions from IRAs or realizing capital gains.

Bucket number three is the rest of your investments—where we would do the tax location planning we previously described. With your first two years of income covered, you now have the freedom to maintain a more strategic long-term portfolio that includes the remainder of your assets. This enables you to capture the various premiums that the investment markets can deliver without upsetting the long-term portfolio for short-term income or cash flow needs. This portfolio would be allocated based on your need, willingness, and ability to accept risks. We'll discuss this more in a later chapter on the investment process. Annually you would use income, rebalancing, or tax loss/gain trading to replenish the short-term portfolio (the second bucket) in a tax-aware manner.

Phase One Distributions

From a tax standpoint, your distributions from the long-term to the short-term portfolio consist of two distinct phases. Phase one begins when you stop receiving a paycheck at retirement. Phase two begins when you are legally required to start taking money from your traditional qualified accounts, such as IRAs and 401(k)s. As I write, the tax code requires you to start taking these distributions, whether you want the money or not, at age seventy-two.[85] The government wants to begin taxing these deferred accounts before you die.

In phase one we have significant control over our taxable income, so we're going to use the retirement distribution system (i.e., eat some of our principal) to manage tax brackets. We don't have that level of control while we're still working because we receive a W-2 from a salary, a 1099 from self-employment income, or profit distribution if we own a business. However, once we retire, and especially in the first phase when we're not forced to take IRA distributions, we can exert some control over our tax liability.

The mistake many people make is to view tax planning as a one-year proposition, but what we really want to do is reduce taxes over a multiyear period. While saving taxes this year might feel wise, it may be smart to accelerate income and pay tax earlier at lower brackets. Using these strategies in phase one, we can be in a really low tax bracket. Therefore, we will evaluate Roth conversions to fill up lower brackets. As the name suggests, a Roth conversion is essentially

---

85   As I write this, Congress is debating legislation that may move this age back to age seventy-five.

taking a traditional IRA or 401(k), converting it to a Roth IRA, and paying the tax liability now instead of later.

You might ask, "Well, why the heck would I want to do that? That seems counterintuitive. Plus, because of the time value of money, wouldn't it be wise to defer taxes and earn a return on the money that would have gone to taxes?" The short answer is *maybe*. But if you're prepaying the tax at lower rates, and your rate increases (because of tax law changes or your future required IRA distributions), your overall lifetime tax burden could be significantly lower, providing more resources to spend, give, or leave as a legacy. If we just let these 401(k)s or IRAs compound, when we turn seventy-two and we're forced to start taking the money out, we could shift into a much higher tax bracket. So timing is crucial.

If you're pessimistic (or perhaps simply realistic) and you believe your tax rates may be higher in the future, you certainly want to consider converting some money from your traditional IRA to a Roth IRA and filling up these brackets. Did I mention that none of this planning should be done in isolation? Consider the following: If you're under sixty-five and not yet on Medicare, you may get a healthcare premium credit from the Affordable Care Act—if your income is low enough. You may need to compare the value of the premium credit against the long-term benefit of the Roth conversion.

You don't want to just automatically increase your income through a Roth conversion without thinking about the impact. An annual analysis and an evaluation of trade-offs are essential. Once again we see the importance of developing a holistic strategy with your financial advisor.

A Roth IRA conversion almost never makes sense if you must take a taxable distribution from the traditional IRA to pay the tax. You'd need to have adequate non-IRA/401(k) assets available to pay the tax liability created by the conversion. Some readers might also protest, "Why would I want to use up my non-IRA assets?" The short answer is that you're making an investment of those assets (the taxes due) so that you have more funds in the tax-free category (the Roth IRA).

In phase one (prior to seventy-two under current law) we have a great opportunity to manage tax brackets. In general we want to fill up brackets from Roth conversions at favorable tax rates if you're in the 10, 12, or (depending on your circumstances) 22 percent marginal tax brackets. If your income is below a certain threshold, you can also harvest capital gains in a zero percent tax bracket. During your annual planning, you would decide which is more advantageous: filling up brackets with Roth conversions or harvesting gains at the zero percent capital gains rates. I know all of this can sound quite complex and confusing. It illustrates the value of ongoing coaching and advice from a holistic wealth advisor or tax planner.

Bunching Charitable Deductions in Phase One

Recent tax law changes have increased the standard deduction. For a married couple filing jointly in 2022, the standard deduction is $25,900 if you are under sixty-five and $27,300 if over sixty-five. For itemizers, the maximum deduction for state and local taxes is $10,000. (As of early 2022, an increase in this deduction is being debated in Congress.) So if your state and local taxes, your mortgage interest deduction, and your charitable gifts are under these amounts, you won't itemize; you'll just take the standard deduction.

Here's the net effect: many charitable gifts you make aren't saving you taxes because you didn't exceed the standard deduction. For example, if your state and local taxes and your mortgage interest deductions are $10,000 combined, and you write a check to your church for $15,000, that donation won't save you any taxes because you have a $25,900 standard deduction, whether you gave the church that money or not.

A more effective strategy might be to take several years' worth of charitable gifts and put them into a donor-advised fund (DAF). Let's say, for instance, that every year you give $15,000 to charity. Since you're not itemizing, this donation doesn't save you taxes. But you could take $60,000 (four years' worth of gifts) and put it in a DAF as a charitable gift for the current year. A DAF allows you to take a tax deduction in the year of the gift, and since you will be exceeding the standard deduction, you should itemize your deductions in that year. Then annually make $15,000 grants from the DAF to your favorite qualified charities. In our example you would file your return using just the standard deduction in years two through four and repeat the "bunching" of gifts in year five.

According to Will Kenton, "Donor-advised funds offer abundant tax advantages. Unlike private foundations, donor-advised fund holders enjoy a federal income tax deduction of up to 50 percent of adjusted gross income for cash contributions, and up to 30 percent of adjusted gross income for the appreciated securities they donate. When donors transfer assets such as limited partnership interests to donor-advised funds, they can avoid capital gains taxes and receive immediate fair-market-value tax deductions."

Kenton adds, "According to the National Philanthropic Trust, donor-advised funds have become an increasingly efficient method for donating to causes. In 2020, assets held in donor-advised funds rose to $141.95 billion, a 16.2 percent increase from $122.18 billion in 2018."[86]

---

86   Will Kenton, "Donor-Advised Fund," *Investopedia*, July 13, 2021.

You generally don't want to give cash to charity if you have low-basis securities in taxable accounts. It's more effective to give the charity these low-basis securities. For example, if you have $10,000 worth of Apple stock and you give $10,000 a year to your church, don't give the church $10,000 in cash. Instead, give them $10,000 in Apple stock, and then use your $10,000 in cash to buy more Apple stock to replace it. That'll raise your basis in the stock, so when you sell it later, you'll pay less in capital gains taxes. Since the nonprofit is a tax-exempt entity, it can sell the stock immediately without tax liability. Therefore, both you and the charity get to take a free bridge.

Phase Two Distributions

Phase two begins at seventy-two when you're required to take distributions from your traditional IRAs (required minimum distributions, RMDs) and you're collecting Social Security. Another advantage of the Roth IRA is that RMDs are not required. At this point a more effective charitable-giving strategy is to make your donations from your traditional IRA using what's called "qualified charitable distributions" (QDCs) rather than using your nonqualified money or other income. Let's say you have a large IRA and you have to take out $60,000 as your RMD. That money will be added to your ordinary income, and you'll have to pay tax on it. If you then turn around and write a $10,000 check to charity, it will not be deductible unless you are itemizing.

If instead you could have the $10,000 sent directly from your IRA to, say, the Humane Society, that donation reduces your AGI by that $10,000. So instead of paying tax on a $60,000 required distribution, you pay tax on a $50,000 distribution. Plus, you still get the full $27,300 (married and over sixty-five) standard deduction. Even though you're not required to take distributions from your IRA or 401(k) until you're seventy-two, you can still use QCDs beginning at age seventy and a half.

As in phase one, in phase two you can and should do bracket management. Continue to evaluate the wisdom of filling up lower brackets and so on. In phase one we were liberally converting traditional IRAs to Roth IRAs. Now with required IRA income and Social Security income, we may be using distributions, tax-free, from the Roth IRA to keep the bracket from being too high. For example, if you have to take a large RMD from your IRA, you may want to get additional income from your Roth IRA or from taxable accounts to replenish the short-term portfolio. You're still managing your income with the three-bucket approach. You're just replenishing bucket number two from bucket number three using taxable RMDs.

Warning! If you don't take your RMD, you'll have to pay a 50 percent penalty on the amount that you should have taken. If you were required to take $60,000 from your IRA once you were seventy-two and you only took $30,000, that leaves you $30,000 short of the requirement. The 50 percent tax penalty thus costs you an additional $15,000. That's a big incentive to obey the RMD rules. Fortunately, the IRS has been lenient here if the oversight was clearly unintentional. If you discover and correct these problems early enough in the next year, they're likely to work with you. But be aware! Did I mention that working with an advisor who can help you monitor these issues could be helpful?

The Impact on Medicare

If you're over age sixty-five and on Medicare, we want to be careful about your Medicare Part B premium when we talk about any strategy to accelerate income at lower brackets. Why? Because that premium is based on your modified adjusted gross income (MAGI). Therefore, any strategy that accelerates income could cause you to pay higher Part B premiums.

Under current law, the cutoff is $182,000 for a married couple filing jointly. If we exceed this level of MAGI, your Medicare Part B premium begins to go up. While it still may make overall financial sense to accelerate income, fill up tax brackets beyond that amount, and pay higher Part B premiums, in my experience, retired clients hate to do that because the money comes out of their Social Security check every month, and they're reminded of the cost. We would want to have a conversation about the trade-offs, collaborate on a decision, and be aware of the potential impact. This is why having an integrated plan you understand and commit to makes so much sense.

We believe tax aware investment planning should be ongoing. In addition to tax location planning, you want to be thoughtful about *when* you take gains. Are they going to be long term or short term? While being sensitive to trading cost, we also generally recommend harvesting losses throughout the year. They can be used against realized gains, and any you don't use can be carried forward.

Let's Get Specific

To make some of these points more concrete, let's look at a specific example. In March 2020 markets were down significantly. We were in COVID-19 lockdown. Because of our investment philosophy and "rational optimism" (more on this in a later chapter), we stayed fully allocated to each client's specific investment strategy. You certainly don't want to sell quality long-term investments when trading at a "discount" after markets fall. However, this was an opportune time to liquidate some holdings and take realized losses that we could use in the future to offset gains. Since we do not want to be out of the market, we take the proceeds and buy another recommended security in the same asset class but not the same security. Note that you cannot repurchase the same security within thirty days because of what's called the *wash sale* rule. If you do, the capital loss cannot be realized for tax purposes.

But you can harvest losses and still stay invested in a replacement security. The net effect is that we have clients who have these realized paper losses but remained fully invested in the appropriate strategy throughout. In a tax-aware investment process, you would continuously monitor and take advantage of these environments when they occur. For instance, we did similar tax-loss harvesting trades during the recession in late 2008 and early 2009. Because of these losses, some clients may not pay significant taxes on their long-term taxable accounts for some time.

We may also harvest gains, as I mentioned. It might make sense to take some gains at low (or potentially zero) brackets, especially if you think your capital gains rate is going to go up. If you're in a low-income tax year, it may be advantageous to accelerate capital gains. In other words you want to monitor your unrealized long- and short-term gain position in your taxable accounts.

If you own bonds, most of the return is from interest income. However, if you sell bonds that have appreciated in value, this gain is treated as a capital gain, not ordinary income. If you have some bonds with unrealized capital gains, you may be better off selling them and paying the preferred capital gains rates rather than holding them and receiving the higher rate for ordinary income.

The Timing of Roth IRA Conversions

The best time to do a Roth conversion is during a bear market or when markets are correcting. Why? Because you're able to move more shares at low cost. In January 2020 I had clients who wanted to convert $100,000 from traditional IRAs to Roth IRAs. But we counseled them to take a wait-and-see approach. We reminded them they had until December 31 to make the conversion. Then in March markets were down significantly. So the $100,000 securities might now be worth $80,000.

Our clients could still convert $100,000 worth of securities because that was the amount of income they wanted to accelerate, but now they were doing so at much lower prices. Some of those converted securities, since they were converted when markets were much lower, are now worth significantly more. Those clients thus have significantly more money in tax-free holdings inside the Roth IRA.

This detail points to the importance of monitoring. We stay in touch with clients throughout the year to take advantage of opportunities as they arise. We have regularly scheduled reviews and tag clients who are Roth conversion candidates. Thus, when markets drop, we can reach out to determine if we should execute or accelerate a Roth conversion strategy.

We are certainly not trying to time markets. We just know that if markets are lower today than they were six months or a month ago, circumstances are more favorable for a Roth conversion. During bear markets or market corrections, we are likely doing more tax-loss harvesting trades. We're tending the garden every day to be ready when opportunities present themselves.

Buyer Beware

As you enter your second act, be cautious about gimmicky and complex products that propose significant tax savings. As a rule of thumb, simple is usually better than complex. And with some of these more complex and potentially aggressive strategies, you subject yourself to a lot of audit risk.

There are a number of simple tax-credit opportunities if you qualify. These are all written into law and reliable. You would want to work with your tax professional to determine those that *As you enter your second act, be cautious about gimmicky and complex products that propose significant tax savings.* are available and make sense for your unique circumstances. Some of these (e.g., conservation easements) have been aggressively marketed by syndicators and have come under great scrutiny of late, and this raises the risk of an audit.

Remember, we're as concerned about *return on life* as we are about *return on investment.* Do you really want to have an IRS audit occupying space in your brain for two or three years while you're supposed to be enjoying your grandchildren and pursuing the second act of your life? Just as you don't want to be glued to CNBC every day worrying about events over which you have no control, you also don't want to be nervously eyeing your mailbox wondering when you're going to get a letter saying your audit has been resolved. It's an unnecessary complexity. Speaking of which, we'll deal with the risks of complex annuities and insurance products in the chapter "Income for Life."

Health Savings Accounts

If you have the option, and you're not a huge consumer of healthcare, few investments are better than a health savings account (HSA). It has triple tax benefits. It's deductible when the money goes into the account. In 2022 the maximum deductible contribution, if you have family coverage, is $7,300. If you're over fifty-five, you can add $1,000 more. So if you had family coverage, and you contribute $8,300, that could save you about $2,500 in taxes, assuming 24 percent federal and 6 percent state marginal tax brackets.

The second benefit is that the money in the HSA grows tax-deferred like a 401(k). You can pull money out throughout the year to cover your out-of-pocket medical expenses. But if you can afford to, we'd recommend that you let it compound because the third benefit is that when you pull the money out to pay for healthcare expenses, it's tax-free.

So it's deductible going in, it's tax-deferred, and it's potentially tax-free.

Nothing else does that!

As I mentioned, we would generally recommend the following: If you have the ability, pay any out-of-pocket (i.e., those not covered by insurance) healthcare expenses yourself and let the HSA account compound until you retire. At that time use the HSA for healthcare expenses. After sixty-five, the money you pull that you don't spend on healthcare is taxable. But you're likely to need it for healthcare. Recall our note from chapter 5: the Fidelity Retiree Health Care Cost Estimate reports that in 2020 the average retired couple age sixty-five may need about $295,000 saved (after tax) for postretirement health-care expenses. Under current law, if you save your receipts throughout your life and you have bills that you've paid out of your own pocket, you can go into your HSA and pull out funds for reimbursement income tax-free.[87]

So here's a typical strategy: Contribute to your employer-sponsored 401(k) up to the amount matched, max out the HSA, and then, depending on your tax bracket, either go back and contribute funds to a traditional 401(k) (tax deductible now, taxable later) or a Roth 401(k) (nondeductible today, tax-free later) or potentially a Roth IRA outside of your employer—if you qualify. Finally, consider making after-tax contributions to your traditional 401(k) if your plan allows it. Why? Because if you build up after-tax balances in your 401(k), when you separate from your employer (either at retirement or if you change jobs), you can roll your cumulative after-tax contributions to a Roth IRA tax-free. For those who do not qualify for a Roth IRA, this is a good way to get funds in the tax-free "Roth" category when you leave your employer. (This strategy is on the chopping block in recent tax proposals. Consult your tax professional.)

Multigenerational Tax Planning with Qualified Plans

After your death, if you've left your IRA, Roth IRA, or 401(k) to a nonspouse beneficiary, that person must distribute and pay tax (if applicable) on those funds over a period of no longer than ten years. Roth IRA distributions would not be taxable to the beneficiary. Thus, managing tax brackets across generations with a traditional IRA/401(k) could be important. If you're trying to maximize wealth for your entire family, meaning your generation and the generation below you, you'll need to be thoughtful because your children or

---

87   Rules could change, so always consult with a qualified tax advisor.

grandchildren who inherit your traditional IRA could be in a significantly different tax bracket than you are—higher or lower.

Across all these issues, your advisor should be proactive throughout the year. And in a VUCA world, with growing government expenditures and debt, these tax considerations may have even more importance in the future than they have today. Somebody's going to have to pay for this at some point. And without a guide who can help you find the free bridges, you may well end up paying more than your fair share.

In the next chapter, we'll look at how to achieve lifelong financial freedom by creating an income stream that can rise in retirement.

CHAPTER 12

Income for Life

Inflation is when you pay fifteen dollars for the ten-dollar haircut you used to get for five dollars when you had hair.
—SAM EWING[88]

The Retirement Income Challenge

Do you have an investment strategy for tripling your income when you stop receiving a paycheck? Are you aware that, without such a strategy, your retirement income stream is unlikely to sustain your current lifestyle over the long term? If you're like many people I talk to, you may find yourself a bit taken aback by these questions. Sam Ewing's comment about the rising cost of haircuts as we go bald may give us a brief smile, but the underlying reality he describes is no laughing matter. Indeed, some of you may want to put the book down right now so you don't have to confront this uncomfortable topic.

---

88 Sam Ewing, "Pepper ... and Salt," *Wall Street Journal*, November 4, 1997.

Please don't. Given the inevitable challenges posed by inflation, increases in the cost of living, longer life expectancies, escalating healthcare costs, and our greater need for such care as we age, our incomes will need to rise in retirement—which now often constitutes a thirty-year interval, more than one-third of our lives.

Unfortunately, having lived through two significant bear markets and a global pandemic since 2000, many people who were already unprepared for retirement are making investment mistakes because they confuse short-term volatility with long-term risk. As a result they seek the illusion of safety and misperceive the real risk. Volatility is not risk. The permanent loss of capital is risk. The real risk isn't the temporary loss of principal; it's the permanent erosion of purchasing power.

Volatility is not risk. The permanent loss of capital is risk. The real risk isn't the temporary loss of principal; it's the permanent erosion of purchasing power.

Clearly the transition from depositing a monthly check to drawing down on our savings produces a great deal of understandable anxiety. But as FDR pointed out, fear itself is seldom conducive to wise decision-making.

In this chapter I'll clarify how those fears can cause us to underestimate our hero's chief challenge: the erosion of purchasing power after they stop working. More specifically, I'll demonstrate that pursuing a fixed-income strategy in a rising cost world is financial suicide on the installment plan. Given that—if history is any guide—living costs will increase 2.5 times over the course of your second act, my contention that you need to triple your income is not mere hyperbole. It's simple arithmetic. In the sections that follow, I'll clarify how to manage your sources of income and build an investment strategy to help you meet that challenge so that you can live with confidence, dignity, and independence.

Claiming Social Security

Most of my clients know that Social Security will constitute part of their Act 2 income, the part they'll receive from the *government* to complement their own *personal* savings and investments—and their *employer-sponsored* benefits. But many clients are less clear on the following four important issues:

1. Social Security was never intended to be your sole source of support. As of 2021, program benefits represent 33 percent of the average retiree's income.[89]

2. There is no single best practice to follow about when to apply for Social Security. Your unique situation will determine the "optimal" choice. The following are among the many variables you'll need to consider: your health status and life expectancy, your immediate need for income, whether or not you plan to work, your investment temperament, and whether you are married, single, or a surviving spouse.

3. The number of workers paying taxes to support each Social Security beneficiary has been declining steadily over time, so the long-term stability of the program is in question. In 1945, ten years after the start of the program, there were forty-two workers for every retiree. By 1960 the number had shrunk to five workers per retiree—a decrease of 88 percent. Projections suggest that by 2030 the ratio will be 2.4 to 1—a

---

89 "Social Security Basic Facts," Social Security Administration, accessed May 3, 2022, https://www.ssa.gov/news/press/factsheets/basicfact-alt.pdf.

further decrease of 17 percent from the 2010 ratio of 2.9 to 1.[90]

4. The system will be able to pay 100 percent of promised benefits until 2034. After that, if nothing is done to reform the program, income will be sufficient to cover just 79 percent of promised benefits.

Given that a married couple has many options for claiming Social Security benefits, my aim here is not to provide an exhaustive analysis of all the possible trade-offs. You wouldn't keep reading if I did. To explore the nuances of your situation, you need to sit down with a financial advisor. That's especially important if you're divorced, a surviving spouse, or if you're married and both you and your spouse have Social Security benefits. You could choose various strategies that allow you to claim on one benefit now, defer the other, and then switch to the larger one later.

As an incentive to meet with a guide, consider that a recent study at the University of Michigan's Retirement and Disability Center revealed that an astounding 22 percent of retirees regret the Social Security decisions they've made.[91] Since these decisions are permanent, that means close to one in four retirees will live out the rest of their lives hurting from the consequences of their mistakes.

One fact I will highlight is that *when* you apply for benefits, it can have an enormous impact on your long-term income. The key

---

90 "Worker-to-Beneficiary Ratio in the Social Security Program,"
    Peter G. Peterson Foundation, May 3, 2019, https://www.pgpf.org/
    chart-archive/0004_worker-benefit-ratio.

91 María J. Prados and Arie Kapteyn. 2019. "Subjective Expectations, Social Security
    Benefits, and the Optimal Path to Retirement." Ann Arbor, Michigan. University of
    Michigan Retirement and Disability Research Center (MRDRC) Working Paper;
    MRDRC WP 2019-405 (https://mrdrc.isr.umich.edu/publications/papers/pdf/wp405.
    pdf).

point to grasp here is what's called your "full retirement age" (FRA), at which you can claim full, unreduced benefits (i.e., your "primary insurance amount" or PIA). FRA used to be sixty-five for everyone, but that number has been going up. For everyone born between 1943 and 1954, FRA is now sixty-six. For everyone born in 1960 and later, FRA is sixty-seven. For those born between 1955 and 1959, FRA is sixty-six plus some number of months. Consult the Social Security Administration's website for more precise details.

If you claim benefits *before* FRA, your monthly check will be reduced according to the age at which you apply.

Figure 12.1 Full retirement and age sixty-two benefit by year of birth.

Year of Birth [1]	Full (normal) Retirement Age	Months between age 62 and full retirement age [2]	AT AGE 62 [3]			
			A $1000 retirement benefit would be reduced to	The retirement benefit is reduced by [4]	A $500 spouse's benefit would be reduced to	The spouse's benefit is reduced by [5]
1943-1954	66	48	$750	25.00%	$350	30.00%
1955	66 and 2 months	50	$741	25.83%	$345	30.83%
1956	66 and 4 months	52	$733	26.67%	$341	31.67%
1957	66 and 6 months	54	$725	27.50%	$337	32.50%
1958	66 and 8 months	56	$716	28.33%	$333	33.33%
1959	66 and 10 months	58	$708	29.17%	$329	34.17%
1960 and later	67	60	$700	30.00%	$325	35.00%

1. If you were born on January 1st, you should refer to the previous year.
2. If you were born on the 1st of the month, we figure your benefit (and your full retirement age) as if your birthday was in the previous month. If you were born on January 1st, we figure your benefit (and your full retirement age) as if your birthday was in December of the previous year.
3. You must be at least 62 for the entire month to receive benefits.
4. Percentages are approximate due to rounding.
5. The maximum benefit for the spouse is 50 percent of the benefit the worker would receive at full retirement age. The percent reduction for the spouse should be applied after the automatic 50 percent reduction. Percentages are approximate due to rounding.

Source: https://www.ssa.gov/benefits/retirement/planner/agereduction.html

If you claim after your FRA, your check will be increased by 8 percent for each year you delay until age seventy—at which point there is no advantage in further delays. For example, a person born in 1960 with a PIA of $3,000 and an FRA of sixty-seven would thus receive $2,100 per month if they applied at age sixty-two but $3,779 if they waited until age seventy—an increase of 80 percent over what they would receive if claimed at sixty-two. Over the course of a year, the person who applied early would receive $25,200. The person who applied at seventy would receive $45,348. The differences become even more dramatic if we multiply these amounts by annual cost-of-living adjustments. It might be hard to pass up Social Security checks when you can start receiving them as early as age sixty-two. But if you can afford to do so—and you live a long time—you'll be glad you waited.

Confusing Certainty with Safety

As you enter Act 2, you have a choice about *when* you want to face financial uncertainty. You can have relative certainty today by putting all your money in fixed-income investments such as bonds. But given historical trends, you're going to have a lot of uncertainty in the future. Why? Because those investments that look "safe" today may not keep pace with inflation. If that happens, you'll have to lower your living standard to keep from running out of money.

On the other hand, you could face more uncertainty today by investing some of your money in assets that may fluctuate in value but that have reliably provided a rising income stream over time. You'll thus have less uncertainty in the future because the return of these asset classes has historically exceeded inflation, and you are thus less likely to deplete your assets.[92]

One of my missions as a wealth manager is to help overcome a bias in many investors who see investing in a globally diversified portfolio of stocks as risky—as if those investments were akin to gambling their money at a racetrack instead of owning a small piece of the world's great businesses. I believe that by owning such businesses, you are harvesting the growth in the global economy. Being a shareholder in these companies has historically been a reliable way to create a rising income stream. The table below clarifies my point.

Figure 12.2 Let markets work for you.

Date	S&P 500	Dividends	Consumer Price Index*
1/1947	15.21	.71	21.50
12/2021	4674.77	60.40	278.73
Compounded Growth Rate	8.05%	6.19%	3.52%

Source: Stock Market Data Used in "Irrational Exuberance" Princeton University Press, 2000, 2005, updated by Robert J. Shiller; updated at http://www.econ.yale. edu/~shiller/data.htm

Over the seventy-four-year period from 1947 through 2021, dividends on the S&P 500 grew from $0.71 a share to more than $60 a share. That's a compounded growth rate of 6.19 percent. Keep

---

92   Past performance is no guarantee of future results.

in mind that this figure totally ignores the underlying value of the business: it's just the profit management has paid out to shareholders in dividends. During that same interval, the consumer price index (a proxy for inflation) grew at 3.52 percent. Thus, income from dividends outstripped inflation by 2.67 percent.

To be clear, I'm not blindly promoting a high-dividend-paying equity strategy. Nor am I advocating a portfolio of 100 percent stocks. Most investors need fixed-income investments in their portfolios to play defense during volatile periods, just as they need equities to play offense against inflation. My point here is that if the goal is the accretion of purchasing power, stocks are safer than bonds as a long-term investment. If the cancer I'm trying to cure is the need for rising income, being a shareholder in the world's great businesses must be part of the answer.

Caution: Don't "Reach for Yield"

As they approach retirement, investors often make the mistake of thinking they should put most of their money in high-dividend-paying stocks, closed-end funds, or high-yield bonds. Reaching for yield is a mistake for "income investors." They imagine they will live off the interest or dividends—and never sell the securities. But it doesn't matter if the return comes from a dividend or a capital gain. The only thing that matters is whether the instrument has reasonable returns. If you own a security that grows from $100 to $110, and you sell 5 percent to live on, that's no different from owning a $100 security with a 5 percent yield and taking the dividend, except that the capital gain may be taxed more favorably if the dividend is not "qualified."

The danger today is that interest rates are so low many people are taking more risks to get higher yields. Many investors are leaving banks and going to treasury bonds, investors in treasury bonds are moving to higher-yielding corporate bonds, and investors in corporate bonds are moving to dividend-paying stocks. That's a mistake. Why? Not only are they taking additional risks, since everyone wants high yield, but also the price of some of these high-yield instruments has been bid up. Consequently "high-yield" instruments have some of the lowest expected returns.

We're more interested in investing in securities that have high expected returns. In a broadly diversified portfolio of quality investments, you are going to get current yield, but that's just a by-product. We'll talk more about how to structure a portfolio in chapter 14, but for now be wary of high-yield instruments because there is no free lunch!

Beware of Extrapolating from Past Returns

As you're building your retirement income plan, be wary about extrapolating from past returns. Many financial advisors and off-the-shelf software packages mechanically plug in historical data—using bond, stock, and cash returns for the last forty years—without taking into account present-day considerations that should temper their expectations.

So for example, they may project bond returns based on what happened since 1980, without taking into account that interest rates on ten-year government bonds have fallen from 15 percent to 1.5 percent over this period. That's like basing your assumption of how the New York Yankees will do this year on how they did when they had Babe Ruth and Lou Gehrig in the lineup. Those guys are long gone, and so are economic circumstances that led to higher returns for bonds.

At the time of this writing, US equities are also historically "expensive." Since expected returns are related to the price you pay for an investment, it is dangerous to assume that recent returns are a good estimate for future returns.

As Mark Twain is reputed to have said, history may rhyme, but it never simply repeats itself. So as you develop a plan to triple your income in retirement, be sure you align your expected returns with the current environment, not on mirage-inducing assumptions that no longer apply. That's true whether the reality-altering changes occurred last month, last year, or last decade.

"Beware of Geeks Bearing Formulas"[93]

The financial services industry will reliably provide products that purport to give investors what they want. Be careful what you wish for. Be especially wary of complex deferred variable annuities with guaranteed income riders that have high internal costs. The internal cost may be so high and expected returns so low that you're likely to get nothing more than the guaranteed minimum rate. My argument has always been that the actuaries at insurance companies are smarter than we are. And if they're aggressively selling products with a three-hundred-page prospectus about how they calculate their guarantees, you should probably run.

I'm not entirely opposed to guaranteed *immediate income* annuities in which you invest a lump sum and receive a paycheck for the rest of your life. Those can be fine for a portion of some portfolios, especially for those who haven't saved enough money and are worried about outliving their capital. But beware trying to increase

---

93   This quote is from Buffett's 2009 letter to his shareholders. For more information, visit https://management.curiouscatblog.net/2009/02/28/ warren-buffetts-letter-to-shareholders-2009/.

your lifetime income with *deferred variable* annuities with complex and expensive riders. As with miracle diets and those lessons that promise to teach you French in a week, there's a reason these financial products sound too good to be true.

In the next chapter, we'll focus on wealth transfer and legacy planning.

CHAPTER 13

Legacy Planning

*The things you do for yourself are gone when you are gone, but
the things you do for others remain and become your legacy.*
—KALU NDUKWE KALU[94]

The Head and the Heart

Years ago I heard a story about a curmudgeonly and somewhat
vulgar old fellow who visited his financial advisor to discuss legacy
planning—sometimes called *estate planning* or *wealth transfer*. The
advisor began, as I do, by trying to determine how his client wanted
to pass on the money and assets he'd accumulated over his lifetime.

Did he want to bestow them on his family?

"Hell no!" the man said. "They'll just … [throw][95] it away on
trivialities!"

---

94   Kalu Ndukwe Kalu, *Citizenship: A Reality Far from Ideal* (New York: Palgrave
      Macmillan, 2009).

95   In the version of the tale I heard, the man replaces "throw" with a vulgar synonym for
      "urinate."

"Okay," the advisor says, "no family." He thinks for a moment and asks, "What about your church?"

Again the client says, in an angrier tone, "Hell no! The church is worse than my family. They'll just [throw] it away on projects that have nothing to do with spirituality."

"Got it," the advisor says. "No family. No church. What about the government?"

For a third time, the client says, his temper rising, "Hell no! The government is the worst of all. They'll just [throw] it away on programs that do more harm than good."

At this point the exasperated advisor begins to lose patience and says, "Look, your estate needs to go somewhere, so you have to decide who gets to throw it away."

The essence of estate planning thus involves sharpening and formalizing those preferences so that the transfer occurs legally and smoothly and so that your heirs are prepared to become the next stewards of your estate.

I'm being facetious here, of course. I've never worked with anyone as cynical as the man in this story. Most of us are eager to pass on our assets and have clear preferences about where they should go. The essence of estate planning thus involves sharpening and formalizing those preferences so that the transfer occurs legally and smoothly and so that your heirs are prepared to become the next stewards of your estate.

In this chapter we'll talk about how your legacy planning involves both the head and the heart—cold logic and your core values. We'll look at issues such as choosing the right executor, preparing all the essential legal documents, specifying who will receive what, monitoring your plan over time, and discussing that plan with your beneficiaries. Throughout we'll keep in mind the bedrock wisdom of the ancient Greek statesman and general Pericles: "What you leave behind is not what is engraved in stone monuments, but what is woven into the lives of others."[96]

The Heart Guides the Head

To use the paradigm in the title of this book, I find that when most people begin planning their legacy, questions of *meaning* precede those of *money*—the heart guides the head. This makes perfect sense: you have to know who and *what* you prize before you can start deciding *how* to apportion your estate. The heart journey focuses on three basic questions: How do you want to bless your heirs? How do you want to influence society? What values should guide your estate plan? For example, if you have young children, determining who's going to raise them trumps just about any other decision you will make. That's a nonfinancial issue.

The head journey concerns how best to achieve what the heart wants: reducing administrative friction, maximizing efficiency, and minimizing taxes and other costs. If you're using your heart to choose a guardian for your kids, you're using your head when you calculate who will best manage their finances. In many cases these should be different people with entirely different skill sets.

In building an estate plan, I see a continuum that runs from a simple and suboptimal strategy to a highly complex and theoretically "perfect" plan. I've found that most people are happiest somewhere in the middle of that continuum. At some point the costs and com-

---

96   Jeffrey Thompson, *Flicker to Flame: Living with Purpose, Meaning, and Happiness* (New York: Morgan James Publishing, 2006).

plexity of striving for absolute perfection outweigh the benefits of achieving it.

The renowned child psychologist D. W. Winnicott made an analogous point about child-rearing. Those parents who strove to be perfect typically ended up being frustrated themselves and raising frustrated children. Winnicott's famous phrase for his own ideal was the unlofty-sounding "good enough" parent—neither intrusive and overbearing nor neglectful and remote.[97]

He wasn't advocating a quest for mediocrity; quite the contrary, he was pointing out that the best results occurred when the parents resisted making a fetish of perfection. In my own field, the "good enough" estate plan (which still requires a great deal of work) tends to produce the happiest clients. We work hard to achieve an effective strategy but forgo the inevitable life-souring distress that comes from the fanatical pursuit of that largely unattainable perfect plan.

Estate Planning Exercise

During an initial estate planning meeting, my first goal is to identify all the players. I want to establish a record of your entire family—your children, grandchildren, and in-laws—along with their dates of birth, contact information, and any special needs they may have. If your cousins, aunts, uncles, or friends are potential heirs, I want to know them as well. I also want to know all the institutions that mean something to you (e.g., church, synagogue, mosque, charities, schools, hospitals). Finally, I want to know everyone on your team (e.g., lawyers, CPAs, advisors).

---

97   D. W. Winnicott, *Playing and Reality* (Milton Park, Abingdon-on-Thames, Oxfordshire: Routledge Press, second edition, 2005).

Once I've established that detailed foundation, I work through this exercise, using the figure below as a guide. Although I've chosen a $5 million estate in this example, the precise amount isn't crucial and will vary from client to client based on what I know about their finances. The key assumption is that clients have absolute control over who gets the money.

They can divide it in any amount they choose—among family, friends, government, or charity. By the time we finish, the clients and I both have a general idea of how they would like their estate distributed. With that established, we can start to move confidently forward with specific goals—keeping in mind that we can revise these choices should circumstances change. In this exercise I ask clients to make dollar allocations, not percentages since the latter can often lead to confusion.

Figure 13.1 Ideal distribution of resources.

Hypothetically, if you had a $5,000,000 estate at the end of your lives (the second death if married), what would your ideal distribution be? Is the next steward prepared?		
Friends, family, etc.	**Charities & Causes**	**Federal Government (taxes)**

Then we can move through a four-step process. First we work with an estate planning attorney to *design* a plan based on the goals and constraints we've established. Next, we *implement* the plan by getting all the legal documents in place and the accounts and beneficiary designations titled properly—transferring ownership if that's appropriate. Then we periodically *monitor* the situation to make sure the plan is still relevant to your goals and family circumstances—and consistent with current tax law. Finally, we get to the *funding* phase when you begin making lifetime gifts or pass away.

Three Ways to Pass on Assets

You can pass on your estate in three ways.

1. Naming one or more *designated beneficiaries* to receive the benefit of a life insurance policy or the balance in retirement accounts, such as a 401(k), an IRA, or an annuity.

2. Transferring assets through *operation of law* (i.e., how the account is titled). For example, with "joint tenants with right of survivorship," the co-owner of an account or a piece of property takes legal possession of that asset when the other co-owner dies. A "payable-on-death designation" passes the account directly to the named beneficiary. Property owned by a trust would pass the property according to the terms of the trust document.

3. Transferring assets through the *probate* process, which typically refers to the administering of your will. Any asset not covered in 1 or 2 above goes through probate.

These three elements must be carefully coordinated so they aren't out of sync or working at cross purposes. You may spend a lot of money and go through a lot of effort to draft a very detailed will or trust, but if all of your assets are passed through beneficiary designations or are distributed by how the property is titled, the will or trust won't affect those assets at all. In that case your final wishes may never be realized, and your careful legacy plans might just as well be sheets of blank paper.

Essential Documents

An audit by a financial advisor can be helpful here. That means running through a hypothetical probate situation to ensure all the key legal documents are in order and that your estate plan will not be compromised by inconsistencies. To use the theatrical metaphor that runs throughout the book, this audit is the equivalent of a dress rehearsal to eliminate any glitches that might spoil the final scene of your closing act. Your advisor should discuss the following, all of which are designed to ensure that the right people receive your bequest at the right time with the least friction:

1. *Power of attorney for healthcare.* In this document you name someone you trust (i.e., your "agent") to make healthcare decisions on your behalf if you are physically incapacitated or lose mental competence.

2. *Power of attorney for financial matters.* This document is similar to number one but applies (as its name suggests) to financial matters only. You are giving someone (the holder of the power) the authority to make financial decisions just as you could yourself. These powers may be *durable* or *springing*.

   - A durable power goes into effect the moment you sign the document and remains so until the end of your life (or until you revoke it). It is generally used when a married couple wants to grant the authority to act on each other's behalf.

   - A springing power of attorney goes into effect (i.e., "springs into action") only if you're physically or mentally unable to make decisions for yourself.

Generally a springing power requires a medical professional to make a determination of your incapacity.

3. *Living will (also known as an "advanced directive for healthcare").* This document differs from what we think of as a "last will and testament" in that it focuses solely on the kind of medical care you do and don't want should you be unable to communicate your preferences. Your living will is a backup to your power of attorney for healthcare. It can help guide your agent by specifying your desire to pursue or avoid specific procedures such as cardiopulmonary resuscitation to extend your life.

4. *Will.* This document allows you to distribute your property in accordance with your wishes and to specify who will care for any minor children. If you die without a will, the state makes decisions according to a formula over which you have no control and could impose unnecessary financial, emotional, and legal burdens on your heirs. The will appoints a personal representative or executor to handle your affairs during the probate process. If you want to put rules around the dissemination of your property, you would create a testamentary trust (and name a trustee) to enforce those rules.

5. *Revocable living trust.* This document allows you to transfer property into a separate legal entity (i.e., the revocable trust), which will own the property during your life. Therefore, at your death, you avoid the costs, complexities, and public exposure of probate because you've already transferred your assets to this new entity. Because the trust is "revocable," you can change it at any point in your life. Consult your attorney to determine if this kind of trust serves your interests.

6. *Irrevocable trust.* Here you relinquish all ownership rights to the assets. Think of it as a gift. Once you give it away, it's gone. As its name suggests, an irrevocable trust (generally) cannot be changed. Speak with an attorney or a CPA about potential tax or creditor protection benefits from an irrevocable trust. Such benefits are unavailable from revocable trusts.

7. *HIPAA release.* This legal document allows your health information to be disclosed to a third party. The waiver is one of a number of patient-privacy measures spelled out in the Health Insurance Portability and Accountability Act (HIPAA) of 1996. This release is important so that your family, your attorney, and others can access your health records in the event of a medical emergency. This document can be especially important if you have young adult children who still rely on you if they need medical attention.

In preparing all of these documents, be sure to work with an estate planning specialist. If you are going in for an operation, you want a surgeon who specializes in the procedure you need, someone who does this work hundreds of times per year. Apply that same logic here. Don't hire a lawyer who does real estate closings all day long. You want someone with particular expertise in estate planning. At my firm, we use our integrated advisor network to collaborate with those professionals with the expertise required.

Are Your Heirs Prepared?

Larry Swedroe and Kevin Grogan note, "While ... families and their advisors pay great attention to *preparing assets for transition to the heirs,* very little, if any, attention is paid to *preparing the heirs for the assets they will inherit.*"[98] They also note that during the estate transfer process, 70 percent of families lose both their assets and their sense of interpersonal goodwill. The culprit? Lack of communication.

That's why we emphasize that clients spend adequate time preparing the next stewards so they are financially mature enough to understand what's coming to them, what their responsibilities are, and what values you want them to carry forward. We all know cases of young athletes who become rich overnight and end up derailing their lives and going broke because they have no idea how to manage their finances. None of us want to see that happen to our heirs.

Family meetings that focus on both money and meaning can be as crucial as the documents I discussed above to your estate planning process. Some readers may recall the story in Genesis when, on his deathbed, Jacob calls together his grandchildren, Ephraim and Manasseh, to affirm the covenant of Abraham with the next generation. While you may not refer to your ideals as a grandiose "covenant," such rituals are as important now as they were then. These can be as simple as living room conversation or as elaborate as something called an *ethical will*, a personal document to communicate your values, experiences, and life lessons to your family. The *form* the conversation takes is less important than the *fact* that it occurs.

Charitable Planning

In a previous chapter, I discussed social capital (i.e., that which you contribute to society). This is money that you either pay in taxes or direct through charitable-giving strategies. Charitable planning can play a significant role in your estate plan. If you want to support a

---

98   Larry Swedroe and Kevin Grogan, *Your Complete Guide to a Successful and Secure Retirement* (Petersfield, UK: Harriman House, 2019).

charity, you must plan carefully to ensure that your gift is effective from both a tax and an emotional perspective.

Making a charity the beneficiary of your retirement assets can be an effective tax-planning strategy. While a detailed discussion of various charitable strategies is beyond the scope of this book, you may want to explore DAFs, charitable remainder trusts, charitable lead trusts, private foundations, and other strategies that can combine the ability to benefit society with significant income and estate tax benefits.

Advanced Planning

While this chapter does not dig into the complexities of estate tax planning, know that if you are likely to have a "taxable" estate, you'll want to explore more advanced planning and gifting strategies. If you are married and have children from previous marriages you want to benefit, additional trust planning and beneficiary reviews are especially important.

In the next chapter, we'll look at goal-focused and evidence-based investing as opposed to relying on your (unreliable) hunches.

CHAPTER 14

Evidence-Based Investing

The most important thing about an investment
philosophy is having one you can stick with.
—DAVID G. BOOTH[99]

Goals Drive Strategy

Suppose you're in the last group of the Masters Golf Tournament, and you're stepping up to the eighteenth tee in the final round. If you have a two-shot lead, your goal is simply to avoid disaster, so you'll play it conservative and aim for the center of the fairway, laying up a bit short of the ominous sand traps on the left. By playing the percentages and drawing on reliable evidence of what happens when you and others play the hole this way, you know that you'll likely make par—or, at worst, a bogie—and get ready to slip on the coveted green jacket. Whether you win by two strokes or one is irrelevant. "Going for broke" risks everything and gains you nothing.

---

99 Quoted in William G. Hammer, *The 7 Secrets of Extraordinary Investors* (New York: Morgan James Publishing, 2012).

If you trail by a stroke, however, you're going to take a different approach. You'll try to muscle your risky drive beyond the bunkers in the hope that your shorter second shot can get you closer to the pin. Then you're one short putt away from a sudden-death playoff and a chance for victory. If your shot goes awry, you'll have the consolation of knowing you gave it your best. Your goal, after all, was to win, not to protect your second place position.

What does this have to do with evidence-based investing? It's simple. Just as the golfers' different objectives (avoiding a double bogie versus making a birdie) determine their final hole tactics, so your second act goals should drive your investment decisions. In this chapter I'll make clear that outperforming the market—aside from being stupendously difficult—is not a goal. Funding your dreams is. So rather than trying to meet some arbitrary and irrelevant benchmarks with a (generally *shooting*) "star" investment manager, you're much wiser to employ a goal-focused and planning-driven process that looks at the rate of return you need to fulfill those dreams or to partner with a firm whose philosophy is goal-focused and planning-driven as opposed to market-focused and performance-driven.

I realize that Wall Street sales tactics may make this advice sound countercultural, so let me reiterate: "Outperformance" is not a financial goal. Endowing yourself with an income you will not outlive, educating your grandchildren, and leaving meaningful legacies to the people you care about—these are financial goals. The objective of the investment process is to capture the returns needed to accomplish such goals in a low-cost, tax-efficient manner.

If you need a birdie to win, your goal demands that you take certain calculated risks.

If you need a par, that same goal demands that you avoid them.

You and your advisor need to understand the difference.

Demystifying the Equity Markets

Evidence-based investing incorporates decades of rigorous and reliable academic research on how markets work and has provided long-term wealth to patient investors. It draws on empirical data that allows investors in the world's great businesses to benefit from the growth in the global economy and capital markets.

How?

Not by playing a reckless zero-sum game in which they hire a guru to predict (i.e., guess) the handful of assets that will produce the absolute highest returns in the near term but instead by buying and holding a highly diversified portfolio of low-cost funds and rebalancing them periodically.

The evidence-based approach trusts markets as an efficient way to capture market premiums—and thus to provide the lifetime income stream we discussed earlier. The most popular alternative is to have a fund manager speculate on your behalf and try to time the market, which as Chesley Southern notes, "is akin to gambling." She adds that "Research has found that these actively managed investments rarely outperform index funds (those that track the market)." Annual studies of the results of active managers show that few beat their respective benchmarks. For example, Morningstar recently reported that "only 24 percent of all active funds beat the average of their rival index funds in the decade that ended June 2020."[100] In my experience, those who ignore the evidence and seek to beat the market through conventional active management tend to fall further and further behind.

I believe growth in equities is organic because, over time, the value of businesses is driven by aggregate corporate earnings, which, in

---

100 Chelsey Southern, "What is evidence-based investing?" Capital Asset Management, March 16, 2021.

turn, are driven by growth in the global economy. That's the result of people getting up every day and trying to make their lives better. This isn't just a US phenomenon. It's people all over the world trying to live better tomorrow than they live today. They improve their education, get jobs, start businesses, and become producers. And they consume products from businesses all over the globe in order to enhance their lives. Being an owner (i.e., a shareholder) in these businesses allows us to participate in their collective growth.

And as we'll see, there's a significant difference in being a shareholder in these businesses and loaning to them (or to governments) through bonds. We'll also see that evidence-based investing provides reliable criteria (not hunches) about selecting a diverse portfolio that allows us to earn a share of the world's ongoing economic growth.

Your Evidence-Based Investment Journey

To give you a general sense of how the evidence-based investment journey works, I'm going to walk you through the "pillars" of the investment process I've developed at my firm, TandemGrowth Financial Advisors. Whether you decide to work with a professional wealth manager or to proceed on your own, these ideas can provide you with a reliable set of guidelines. And as we discussed in chapter 9, employing a proven process is often the difference between success and failure.

PILLAR 1. GOALS DRIVE INVESTMENT POLICY.

Begin by clarifying your goals and aspirations: What do you want to accomplish in your second act? What would a great life look like? Next, develop actionable plans to reach those goals. To go back to our metaphor of the Masters, are you two strokes up or one stroke down? We need to know that before we can develop the strategies and mix of assets that have a reasonable chance of funding your goals. How much you need to earn will drive your investment policy. Can you meet all your goals with a low-volatility/lower-return strategy? If so, your advisor would be irresponsible to recommend that you accept needless uncertainty.

PILLAR 2. INVEST RATIONALLY, NOT EMOTIONALLY.

This issue is so important that we're going to make it the focus of our next chapter. For now, however, you should understand this key and counterintuitive point: most people fail as investors not because of *intellect* but because of *behavior*. Over a lifetime of investing, I've become convinced that the difference between investors who act logically versus those who act emotionally drives outcomes even more than the investments themselves.

> *Most people fail as investors not because of intellect but because of behavior.*

PILLAR 3. DIVERSIFY BROADLY.

A brilliant and witty author, Mark Twain was a "stupendously incompetent businessperson"[101] who made a ruinous series of investments that turned the nation's most highly paid author into someone struggling to care for his family. So I feel no compunction about disagree-

---

101   Richard Zacks, "The 19th-Century Start-Ups That Cost Mark Twain His Fortune," *Time*, August 19, 2016.

ing with his comment, "The wise man saith, put all your eggs in one basket, and guard the basket."[102]

Contra Samuel Clemens, you should put your eggs in a diverse basket of assets that have different expected returns and that (in general) don't move in the same direction at the same time. The analogy I like is an all-weather garden where something is always in bloom. In most cases, for example, stocks and high-quality bond prices have low correlations and are negatively correlated in many environments. When one goes up, the other tends to go down.[103] For instance, during recessions, when many investors sell stocks and flee to the "perceived" safety of bonds, the value of bonds goes up. Owning some bonds increases your likelihood of enduring a bear market so you can reap the benefits when the bull market returns—as it always has over the long term.

The graph on the next page shows that while various asset classes can zig and zag sharply—often in opposite directions—owners of diversified portfolios follow a smoother path.[104]

---

102 Mark Twain, *Pudd'nhead Wilson* and *Pudd'nhead Wilson's Calendar* (Norwalk, Connecticut: Easton Press, 1998).

103 I'm simplifying a bit: This is a common pattern, not an absolute one.

104 Diversification does not eliminate the risk of market loss.

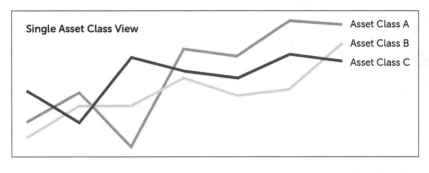

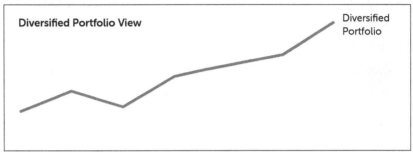

Figure 14.1 A diversified portfolio can provide a more stable outcome.

Keep in mind that I'm talking about diversity both *within* and *among* your investments. On one level, you have asset class diversification, so you'll own, for example, some combination of stocks, bonds, real estate, cash, and other assets. But we also aim for diverse types of stocks, bonds, and so on. That might mean owning short-, intermediate-, and long-term bonds—some issued by governments (federal and state), some issued by corporations. It might also mean owning a range of US stocks, international stocks, and emerging market stocks because no one ever knows which will have their day in the sun next. And you still want to be diversified *within* these categories so you capture the expected returns of the asset class without being ruined if you own too much of one stock such as Enron or Eastman Kodak. Simply put, you will not own enough of any one security to *make a killing*, but neither will you own enough to *be killed*. By holding a globally diversified portfolio, investors are well positioned to capture returns wherever they occur.[105]

There's never been a twenty-year period in our history in which you would have lost money in stocks as an asset class (with dividends reinvested and before inflation).[106] But you'd often have lost *all your money* if you were concentrated in one stock and that company went bust. It's not a risk worth taking. Though I disagreed with Mark Twain earlier, I'm on board with his late-life comment regarding his ill-advised investments: "There are two times in a man's life when he should not speculate: when he can't afford it and when he can." Owing a diversified basket of quality businesses for the long term is not speculating. It is a high-probability endeavor. Concentrating a portfolio on one stock or idea is speculating. So is concentrating a portfolio in one asset class (even if it's gold, cash, or real estate).

Back in the late 1990s, a prospective client told me, "I have a really diversified portfolio. I have these three growth stock mutual funds, and each one of them holds two hundred stocks." But when I dug into those three funds, they were concentrated in large US tech stocks right at the top of the bursting bubble. He was playing Russian roulette and just hoping he never spun a bullet into the live chamber. So just because you own a lot of securities doesn't necessarily mean that you're broadly diversified.

The wisdom of a diversified approach is certainly not a new idea. In Shakespeare's *The Merchant of Venice*—first performed in 1600—the

---

105 For a graphic depiction of the unreliability of trying to pick asset classes by relying on the previous years' "winners," see the asset class returns chart at https://am.jpmorgan.com/us/en/asset-management/adv/insights/market-insights/guide-to-the-markets/.

106 "S&P 500 Historical Return Calculator," DQYDJ, September 7, 2020, by PK (https://dqydj.com/sp-500-historical-return-calculator/).

title character, Antonio, says, "My ventures are not in one bottom [i.e., a ship] trusted / nor to one place; nor is my whole estate / upon the fortune of this present year."[107] More than four centuries ago, Shakespeare knew about diversification!

PILLAR 4. BE SMART ABOUT ASSET LOCATION.

We've discussed the fundamentals of this step in chapter 11 on tax planning. The key idea is to allocate the most tax-efficient asset classes in your portfolio into taxable accounts and the least tax-efficient asset classes into tax-sheltered accounts. For example, you're likely to own bonds and global real estate securities in your portfolio, but ideally you want to own them in tax-sheltered accounts such as an IRA because much of the return comes from dividends and interest taxed at higher ordinary income rates. On the other hand, large US stocks generate most of their returns from more tax-favored capital gains. Generally you would want to own these in your taxable accounts. You should create a list of the asset classes and securities you want to own and then rank them based on their tax efficiency. This will be helpful as you evaluate what to own in which type of accounts.

PILLAR 5. REBALANCE PERIODICALLY AND EMPLOY TAX-AWARE TRADING.

You should periodically rebalance your portfolio to manage risk and to keep you within the allocation levels dictated by your plan, preventing you from getting too skewed to equities or to fixed income. If your plan has dictated a 60/40 ratio of stocks to bonds, and stocks have done well

---

107   William Shakespeare, *The Merchant of Venice*, 1.1.43–45, edited by Alden T. Vaughan and Virginia Mason Vaughan, *Arden Shakespeare*, third ser. London: Bloomsbury, 2011.

over the past year, the weighting of your portfolio may have shifted and thus increased your equity exposure and therefore your risk. Similarly, if stocks have fallen, you may now be overweight to bonds, and your allocation may have not only lower expected volatility but also lower expected returns, which could jeopardize the funding of your goals.

In the next chapter, we'll discuss the behavioral elements that might, at this point, lead you astray, but for now here's the key point: stick with your plan. Rather than doubling down on last year's trend, rebalance by selling some of the higher-performing asset classes and reallocating to your target, which will force you to increase exposure to asset classes that have lagged and are now being offered at bargain prices.

Return to your strategic allocation (e.g., 60/40, 80/20). You don't want to look at your "balanced" portfolio ten years from now and see that you're at a 90/10 stocks to bonds right before a 50 percent downturn.

You may remember the phrase "regression to the mean" from your statistics class. Or you may know that if a baseball player goes 4 for 4 on opening day, he's not going to bat 1.000 or even .400 for the year. Nor is the player who goes 0 for 4 going to bat 0.000. Both are going to regress/progress to something like their lifetime averages.

The same is true in investing: over time, asset classes will gravitate to their average growth rates. Data shows that it's impossible to predict which classes will outperform others from year to year, so rather than trying to predict (or time) a "hot streak," keep disciplined and stick with the careful plan that's designed to achieve your goals. Try to automate this process as much as possible so that you eliminate judgment because it's likely to be emotionally difficult to sell assets that have just gone up (sell high) and buy those that have just gone down (buy low). Like Odysseus's disciplined sailors, block out the alluring but ultimately ruinous siren songs and stay on course.

As I've just pointed out, if an asset class has had a long summer, at some point it's going to have a winter. But that summer can last a long time. If we rebalance too often, we may miss out on positive momentum and could incur taxes and transaction costs. As my podcast cohost Mike Bernard often says, your investments tend to be like bars of soap: the more you handle them, the smaller they get.

At my firm, we rebalance at strategic points throughout the year using tolerance bands derived from academic research. In our process we look frequently (using sophisticated software) but seek to trade infrequently. This approach allows us to capture some short-term momentum without incurring undue risk. For instance, if we have a 10 percent allocation to emerging market stocks, we put a 25 percent band around rebalancing. So we wouldn't sell any of it unless it was up to 12.5 percent or more, and we wouldn't buy more unless it was at 7.5 percent or less.

But if you don't have an advisor, you'll capture most of the benefit if you rebalance once a year. That way you're not incurring significant transaction costs or creating a lot of tax liability. The key is to maintain a fixed schedule, make the process rules-based, and resist the urge to forecast.

You should also monitor your portfolio periodically for opportunities to harvest losses that could be used against future gains. As we discussed in chapter 11, if you're in a low-income year, you might even "harvest" gains at favorable tax rates.

PILLAR 6. SELECT THE APPROPRIATE INVESTMENT VEHICLE.

Much of the financial industry starts here with large advertisements and marketing campaigns to sell investment products. Although you can big mistakes at this point, low-cost, tax-efficient investment vehicles are readily available to investors of all sizes. I believe that the best solutions are those that use an evidence-based approach—buying products that rely on rigorous, peer-reviewed academic research—a topic to which we will devote the rest of this chapter.

Let Markets Work for You

The competitive market and costs work against traditional actively managed mutual fund managers who try to "outperform" through stock picking or market timing: only 19 percent of US-based equity mutual funds and 11 percent of fixed-income funds have survived and outperformed their benchmarks over the past twenty years.[108]

Figure 14.2 Few actively managed equity funds have survived and outperformed. Source: Mutual Fund Landscape 2021: A Study of US-Based Mutual Fund Performance (Austin: Dimensional, 2021).

We've also seen that past performance offers little insight into a fund's future returns. For example, from 2010 to 2020, only 21

---

108 All statistics and graphs in this section are from *Mutual Fund Landscape 2021: A Study of US-Based Mutual Fund Performance* (Austin: Dimensional, 2021).

percent of equity funds and 30 percent of fixed-income funds with returns in the top quartile of the previous five years maintained a top-quartile ranking in the following five years.

On the other hand, the financial markets have rewarded long-term investors. People expect a positive return on the capital they supply, and historically the equity and bond markets have provided growth that has more than offset inflation. The graph below shows that a dollar invested in small company stocks in 1926 would be worth roughly $37,000 today. For large company stocks, the figure is about $14,000. Long-term government bonds and cash would be worth $194 and $22, respectively.[109]

---

109 This and the next graph: In USD. US Small Cap is the CRSP 6–10 Index. US Large Cap is the S&P 500 Index. US Long-Term Government Bonds is the IA SBBI US LT Govt TR USD. US Treasury Bills is the IA SBBI US 30 Day TBill TR USD. US Inflation is measured as changes in the US Consumer Price Index. CRSP data is provided by the Center for Research in Security Prices, University of Chicago. S&P data © 2022 S&P Dow Jones Indices LLC, a division of S&P Global. All rights reserved. US long-term government bonds and Treasury bills data provided by Ibbotson Associates via Morningstar Direct. US Consumer Price Index data is provided by the US Department of Labor Bureau of Labor Statistics. Past performance is no guarantee of future results.

Figure 14.3 Growth of wealth of broad asset classes.

Growth of Wealth:
Monthly: 1/1/1926 - 12/31/2021

	$1 Grew to:	Compounded Returns:
Small Cap	$37,487	11.59%
S&P 500 Index	$14,076	10.46%
LT Corporate Bonds	$298.15	6.11%
LT Gov't Bonds	$194.28	5.64%
One Month Treasury Bills	$21.72	3.26%
Inflation (CPI)	$15.58	2.90%

Obviously it's been a lot more profitable to be a *shareholder* in the world's great businesses than to be a *lender*. Therefore, the most important decision you're going to make as you design your portfolio is how much you have in equity investments (stocks and real estate) versus the fixed-income investments (bonds and treasury bills).

As we discussed in the retirement income chapter, what really matters is not your *nominal* return but rather your *real* return after inflation. And as you can see from the chart below, on an after-inflation basis, equities have provided almost three times higher returns than bonds. This makes sense, as equities are real businesses, with products, plants, and equipment. As prices rise, these assets tend to appreciate in value, and as input prices become more expensive to the business, they can frequently pass these additional costs to the consumer. Bonds, on the other hand, generally pay the investor (lender) a fixed rate regardless of the state of inflation in the economy.

Figure 14.4 Growth of wealth of broad asset classes after inflation.

Growth of Wealth After Inflation:
Monthly: 1/1/1926 - 12/31/2021

	$1 Grew to:	Compounded Returns:
Small Cap after Inflation	$2,407	8.45%
S&P 500 Index after Inflation	$903.73	7.35%
LT Corporate Bonds after Inflation	$19.14	3.12%
LT Gov't Bonds after Inflation	$12.47	2.66%
One Month Treasury Bills after Inflation	$1.39	0.35%

How you allocate your long-term portfolio between stocks and bonds will vary based on your circumstances and goals (i.e., your need, willingness, and ability to accept risks). In the following sections, I'll clarify what evidence-based investing tells us about selecting equity investments.

Sentiment versus Profit

The economist and investor Benjamin Graham wrote, "In the short run, the market is a voting machine; in the long run, it's a weighing machine."[110] His point was that, initially, a stock's value is determined disproportionately by subjective investor sentiment (the voting machine) but that over time the more objective scale (the weighing machine) of corporate earnings becomes the measure that counts.

The chart below illustrates that, in the short term, investor sentiment can overwhelm fundamentals.

Figure 14.5 In the short term, investor sentiment can overwhelm fundamentals.

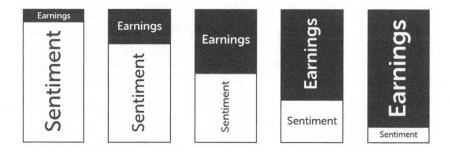

Over time sentiment no longer matters, and the earnings (i.e., profits) drive the results. The voting machine is now a weighing machine. Evidence-based investing focuses on the objective weight, not the erratic votes of *Mr. Market*.[111]

Three Investment Philosophies

We've already seen that conventional asset management—trying to outguess the market through the research and stock picking of an expert manager—simply has low odds of success for the vast majority

---

110   Benjamin Graham, *The Intelligent Investor: The Definitive Book on Value Investing. A Book of Practical Counsel* (New York: Harper Business, revised edition, 2006).

111   Cory Mitchell, "Mr. Market," Investopedia, June 25, 2019 (https://www.investopedia.com/terms/m/mr-market.asp).

of investors. In essence your success in this philosophy depends on your ability to pick the winning managers and avoid the losers.

As Charles Ellis points out, fifty years ago you may have had a chance because your competition was other individuals like yourself; today you're competing against high-powered institutions run by people coming out of Stanford and Wharton.[112] You're competing against Warren Buffett. And you aren't going to win that game any more than you are going to beat Roger Federer at tennis. Your odds of winning are so low that the conventional game isn't worth playing.

Larry Swedroe makes a similar point: "There's no doubt that the competition is much tougher now, even compared with the 1990s. Today pretty much everyone is an MBA or PhD in finance. They're all armed with the latest academic research, high-powered computers, and they are working at firms that hire world-class scientists and mathematicians. Where is your advantage? It's really incredible to think that people like you or me are going to beat these people at the game.... But somehow investors think they're going to compete, and the odds of that are incredibly small."[113]

How small? In 2021 Swedroe notes that "only about 2 percent of actively managed funds generate statistically significant alphas [i.e., an ability to outperform the market] on a pre-tax basis."[114] Moreover, even if you manage to pick the high-performing managers, your results are likely to be disappointing because they cost too much. As Cliff Asness wryly comments, sometimes your wins end up being

---

112 Charles Ellis, *Winning the Loser's Game: Timeless Strategies for Successful Investing* (New York: McGraw Hill, eighth edition, 2021).

113 Dan Bortolotti, "Is beating the market harder than ever?" *MoneySense*, August 10, 2015.

114 Larry Swedroe, "The Odds of Outperforming through Active Management," The Evidence-Based Investor, February 24, 2021 (https://www.evidenceinvestor.com/the-odds-of-outperforming-through-active-management/).

losses: "There is no investment so good that there isn't a fee large enough to kill it."[115]

A "passive" alternative to the conventional approach is to build a portfolio whose holdings mirror those of *a particular index* (e.g., the S&P 500, Russell 2000, Wilshire 5000, Nasdaq Composite). Index funds seek to meet the returns of a specific market, on the assumption that, over time, it will outperform most traditional active managers at much lower cost. So rather than trying to pick a few specific winners, an index investor owns the entire market.

One of the disadvantages of this approach is that it's still actively managed to an extent: a committee is getting together once or twice a year to decide which companies come into the index and which companies go out. In addition, commercial index products tend to produce a portfolio heavily weighted to the largest, most popular, most expensive companies. Why? Because the weightings of the holdings are determined by their market capitalization (i.e., price × outstanding shares). This can result in a fairly concentrated portfolio of the most popular stocks with positive momentum and high prices.

Why is that a problem? In the late 1990s, the indexes were dominated by large technology stocks right before the tech bubble burst. In 2006 and 2007, one of the largest sectors was financial stocks right before the financial crisis.

The third alternative is the one I'm advocating: evidence-based investing, in which you follow the academic evidence about selection criteria and overweight securities that have higher expected returns. The research identifies "factors" or "characteristics" of securities that produce higher expected returns. With the advent of more robust data and computing power, many factors have been identified. However,

---

115   "Go with the Flow(s)," Evidence Based Investing, March 31, 2017 (https://ebi.co.uk/
      evidence-based-investing/go-with-the-flow-s/).

there are only a few that you should focus on; factors you can trust must be:

1. *Sensible.* The underlying logic is evident. It should make intuitive sense. There's no smoke and mirrors. For instance, if you mined the data and found that companies that start with the letter *F* outperformed all other stocks, you would not trust this "factor."

2. *Persistent across time.* When you examine the data, the factor produced positive results over different intervals.

3. *Pervasive across markets.* If the factor explains how markets work, it should hold true in the United States, other developed countries, and emerging economies.

4. *Evident regardless of how you measure it.* Trustworthy factors should be evident using various measurement criteria. Thus, for example, the *value factor* should produce a positive outcome regardless of how you assess value (i.e., whether you're using price-to-book, price-to-earnings, price-to-cash-flow, or other yardsticks).

5. *Cost-effective to capture in well-diversified portfolios.* If it is too costly to implement, the benefit of the strategy can be offset by these costs.

While I continue to review new research on potential new factors, I believe most investors could add value to the traditional "market cap weighted" portfolio by focusing on the factors discussed below.

Factors Linked to Higher Expected Returns

There is a wealth of academic research into what drives returns. While I realize this may be a different approach for many who either rely on unreliable active managers or default to market cap weighted indexes, investors can use this information to pursue higher expected returns in their portfolios. By simply over-weighting (or tilting) their equity investments to these factors, you would have historically earned higher returns.[116]

> *To increase expected returns, increase exposure to stocks over bonds.*

1. *Stocks beat bonds (a.k.a. the market premium).* In US markets, this proves true 70 percent of the time at one-year intervals, 78 percent at five-year intervals, and 86 percent of the time at ten-year intervals. In non-US developed markets the corresponding figures are 62, 71, and 94 percent. In emerging markets, they are 64, 75, and 82 percent. Thus, to increase expected returns, increase exposure to stocks over bonds.

2. *Small beats large (a.k.a. the small-cap premium).* Over time small company stocks have outperformed large company stocks. As we've seen, a dollar invested in large company stocks in 1926 would be worth approximately $14,000 today, whereas the same dollar invested in small company stocks would have grown to approximately $37,000. The excess return of small company stocks over those from large companies is referred to as the "small-cap premium." Having exposure to *small-value stocks* (i.e., smaller companies with low prices relative to economic fundamentals) has historically

---

116   Information provided by Dimensional Fund Advisors LP.

yielded even higher returns. A dollar invested in such stocks in 1927 would have grown to approximately $150,000 today![117] Of course, there is no free lunch here. Small-value stocks are riskier, and therefore, investors require more compensation for accepting this risk. Similarly, small companies are riskier than larger companies, and thus, they compensate investors accordingly.

3. *Value beats growth (a.k.a. the value premium).* Value stocks differ from growth stocks in that they have lower prices relative to economic fundamentals such as book value, earnings, or cash flow. Over time they've also outperformed growth stocks. This is known as the "value premium."

4. *High profitability beats low profitability (a.k.a. the profitability premium).* This one may seem obvious. However, in an efficient market, one would expect that the benefits of higher profitability would already be reflected in the stock price and therefore not offer higher returns. However, the evidence indicates that more profitable businesses do in fact outperform lower-profit businesses if you consider the price paid for the security. There is also a "quality premium," but I believe this is captured using strategies that filter for higher profitability.

5. *Momentum matters (a.k.a. the momentum premium).* In a kind of financial equivalent of Newton's first law, companies in motion tend to stay in motion, and those at rest tend to stay at rest. Stocks that have risen/fallen in the recent past tend to continue to rise/fall for longer than expected.

---

117   Dimensional US Small Cap Value Index. Past performance is no guarantee of future results.

Therefore, a strategy that targets positive momentum stocks and avoids negative momentum stocks can add value.

Investors can pursue higher expected returns through a low-cost, well-diversified portfolio that targets these factors.

A Word about Fixed Income

Fixed-income investments (bonds) can be incredibly complex. There are thousands of securities to consider. As with stocks, traditional active management has not produced encouraging results with fixed-income investments. Plus, with lower expected returns, cost matters even more. As with equities, there are systematic factors in fixed income that are worth exploring as well. You should focus primarily on the term premium, sensitivity to interest rates, credit premiums, and the credit quality of the issuer.

While bonds can be complex, bond math is relatively straight-forward. Evidence indicates that the current yield is a good indicator of subsequent realized returns. In constructing the bond portion of a portfolio, you must evaluate your goal for the bonds. Is it to produce income, for capital appreciation, or to dampen volatility? I believe that most of the volatility and expected returns should come from the equities. Therefore, if you choose to implement a "factor tilt" portfolio as I am discussing here, I encourage you to think of the bonds in the portfolio as "defense" against environments that are bad for stocks. Thus, the primary role of bonds is to dampen volatility so you can stick with your diversified portfolio in good times and bad. The bond allocation would then focus on low-cost products, high quality (little credit risk), and low correlations to stocks.

Why Now?

Since our hero is moving into the second act at a time where expected returns in general could be lower, I believe adopting this evidence-based approach and thus tilting your investments to align with the factors listed above is more important than ever. Readers should keep in mind two important facts: First, as mentioned before, there is no free lunch. Higher expected returns in an asset class or a factor come because they are either riskier or because of behavioral reasons we'll discuss in the next chapter. If they had lower risk or were easy to own, returns would be lower. Second, none of the individual factors works in all environments.

That's why taking a multifactor approach is crucial. You don't want just value or size or profitability or momentum. Since most risk assets have similar expected returns, you want to own a range of them. Just as you want diversification in asset classes, you also want diversification in exposure to these factors.

You can think of evidence-based investing and this multifactor approach in terms of a cross-country drive from New York to Los Angeles. If you let your goals drive your financial plan and determine your ratio of stocks to bonds, that will probably get you all the way to Denver. Then if you implement your portfolio in a diversified way, that might take you to Utah. If you expand your allocation to include small company, international, and emerging market stocks, you'll get to Las Vegas. And finally, if you tilt your portfolio to the academically supported factors we just explored, you'll make it to Los Angeles and the Pacific Ocean.[118]

---

118 I did not invent this analogy, but I've heard it used in a number of talks, and so am unable to specify who was the first to employ it.

And as you drive, you will want to remember the following three overriding principles of every goals-based and planning-driven investor, which I adopted from Nick Murray more than twenty-five years ago:

1. *Faith in the future and the capital markets.* The evidence supports this belief. I've never known a successful investor who lacked this quality.

2. *Patience.* This is a most "un-American" quality. The key, as Kipling said, is the ability "to keep your head / when all about you are losing theirs"[119] and to give a sound strategy time to work.

3. *Discipline.* You must apply the strategy and behaviors consistently over time.

We'll explore these qualities more fully in the final chapter when I discuss behavioral investing and the reasons I'm a rational optimist.

---

119   Rudyard Kipling, "If," *The Collected Poems of Rudyard Kipling* (London: Wordsworth Editions Ltd., 1999).

CHAPTER 15

Behavioral Investing

I can calculate the movement of the stars,
but not the madness of men.
—ISAAC NEWTON[120]

Do the Opposite?

In one of the most memorable episodes on the TV comedy *Seinfeld*, the hapless character George Costanza decides that his decision-making skills are so reliably wrongheaded that he will adopt a new approach: doing the exact opposite of what his gut instinct or initial impulse propels him to do. Accordingly, he walks up to an attractive woman and, rather than trying to impress her, blurts out, "My name is George. I'm unemployed and live with my parents." Infatuated, she begins to date him. At a job interview with the New York Yankees, he candidly reveals the humiliating misbehaviors that have gotten

---

120 Orhan Erdem, *After the Crash: Understanding the Social, Economic and Technological Consequences of the 2008 Crisis* (Cham, Switzerland: Springer Nature Switzerland, 2021).

him fired from his previous two jobs—and then berates the team's irascible owner, George Steinbrenner, for the way he's let down the fans. Rather than calling security, Steinbrenner tells the interviewer, "Hire this man."

I'm certainly not recommending that you model your overall life strategy on George's harebrained inversion of common sense. We laugh, after all, because we recognize its absurdity. But for investors, there is an important kernel of truth hiding amid the laughs. In this chapter I'll try to convince you that human beings are "predictably irrational"[121] and that the key to thriving in what the psychologist Daniel Crosby calls "Wall Street Bizarro World"[122] is to do something that's much harder than it sounds: using our reason to override our emotions, intuitions, egos, and overconfidence—as well as our tendency to credit sensational news headlines over statistical probability and to believe our inaccurate biases about what we "know" with what is actually true.[123]

Our brains have evolved to perform many complex tasks exquisitely well. Unfortunately, investing our money is not one of them. As Nick Murray notes, left unchecked, "Human nature is a failed investor."[124] Just as the hero Odysseus had the foresight to tie himself to the mast so as not to be emotionally seduced by the siren's songs, so this chapter will emphasize that self-restraint and the tempering power of reason are the unglamorous but essential constituents to a successful second act investment strategy.

---

121 Dan Ariely, *Predictably Irrational: The Hidden Forces That Shape Our Decisions* (New York: Harper Press, 2009).

122 Daniel Crosby, *The Laws of Wealth: Psychology and the secret to investing success* (Petersfield, UK: Harriman House, 2021).

123 Readers may want to revisit our chapter 8 discussion of Type 1 and Type 2 thinking as articulated by Nobel Prize–winning psychologist Daniel Kahneman.

124 Evan Simonoff, "Nick Murray: Growth vs Income Delusions Cause Retirement Inequality in an Era of 3-D Hearts," Financial Advisor, May 3, 2019.

As Crosby notes, "Despite the unequivocal truth that investor behavior is a better predictor of wealth creation than fund selection or market timing, *no one dreams about not panicking, making regular contributions, and maintaining a long-term focus.*" My aim is to refocus your dreams in a way that accurately prizes these fundamental virtues.

Closing the "Behavior Gap"

Financial planner and writer Carl Richards coined the term "behavior gap" to describe the disparity between the *higher* organic returns *investments* tend to generate and the *lower* returns *investors* actually receive because of their own emotionally misguided behavior—what Richards bluntly calls "doing dumb things with money."[125] *Morningstar* reports that rates of return for investors were lower (by five basis points per year) than total investment returns over the ten-year period ending on December 31, 2019.[126]

Richards contends that the problem is not with the investments per se but with how people manage them. The following graph depicts the central problem. If you are buying when you are elated because the market is doing well, you're paying high prices and chasing an often unsustainable trend. Conversely if you sell when you are nervous because the market is in a slump, you're receiving low prices and forgoing the likely recovery that historically follows a downturn.

---

125   Carl Richards, *The Behavior Gap: Simple Ways to Stop Doing Dumb Things with Money* (New York: Portfolio Penguin, 2012).

126   Dana Anspach, "What Is the Behavior Gap?" *The Balance*, January 28, 2021.

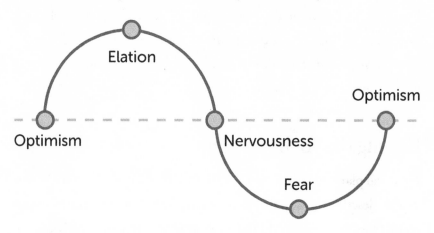

Figure 15.1 Invest rationally, not emotionally.

Recalling George Costanza, you need to mistrust your first instinct in these cases and *do the opposite*—act countercyclical: When markets are high, you should be cautious—because that's when

> **When markets are high, you should be cautious—because that's when expected returns are lowest and markets are riskiest.**

expected returns are lowest and markets are riskiest. When your pattern-seeking brain spots a perceived trend or there is "news," it is likely already in the price. You'll always be late to the party. On the other hand, when markets have declined or are in "bear market" territory, you should be opportunistic: your prospects are likely better, and expected returns are higher. The last thing an accumulator of shares should want is for markets to go up.

The Financial Media

We have an enemy in our quest to invest rationally and not emotionally. That enemy is the financial media. It is my sad duty to report that financial journalism is not in business to make you wealthy but to sell advertising and therefore get an audience. The principles discussed in this book can help you accomplish your lifelong dreams in your second act, but, if executed properly, they make for a boring TV show or magazine article. A financial publication is much more likely to get eyeballs with a catchy title like "The Ten Stocks to Buy *Now!*" Your favorite investment news cable station is likely to get viewers to watch a guest who makes bold predictions no one will track.

A goal-focused and planning-driven strategy is long term because your investment time horizon is your life expectancy. If you retire in your early sixties, this could be more than thirty years. The financial media's sensational stories focus on today. The talking heads want you to feel compelled to tune in and act now, or else you'll miss an opportunity. Rarely should anything happening in markets over a day, a week, a quarter, and possibly even a year alter a well-thought-out investment plan. While these magazines and programs may have some entertainment value, feel liberated to tune out (or at least filter) the noise.

Less Is More

With most activities in life, we are better at forecasting the near future than the distant: You know more about what your workday will entail a day or a week from now than a year from now. You're better able to predict your overall health for tomorrow than for a decade from now. But investing doesn't follow this familiar paradigm. Just as we can rely on the long-term seasonal changes more than we can next week's weather forecast, so we are much better able to predict market trends over the next eight years than over the next eight months.

This insight should give us pause when we feel that we can buy our way into the next hot market trend—or dramatically shift course and sell our way out of the next disaster. The French philosopher Blaise Pascal said that the vast majority of human problems come "from our inability to sit quietly in a room, alone"[127] rather than frantically overreacting to our emotions and taking ill-conceived and impulsive actions, which reliably create more problems than they solve. As we enter our second act, we should adopt a financial equivalent of the physician's Hippocratic oath: "First, do no harm."

Though Pascal was writing in 1654, his diagnosis is spot on for today's hyperactive investors. As Crosby points out, when the Vanguard Group examined the performance of "accounts that had made no changes versus those who made tweaks, ... they found that the 'no change' condition handily outperformed the tinkerers. Further, Meir Statman cites research from Sweden showing that the heaviest traders lose 4 percent of their account value each year to trading costs and poor timing. These results are consistent worldwide: across 19 major stock exchanges, investors who made frequent changes trailed buy-and-hold investors by 1.5 percentage points per year." Less is—consistently and obviously—more. The question is not whether we can *see* that obvious truth but whether we can tamp down our emotions.

Be Rational about Your Irrationality

Most of us are far less rational than we suppose. The key to becoming more logical is to take a "pause" when we feel the need to act and give the System 2 analytical brain we previously discussed a chance to consider the impact on your goal-focused financial plan. It can also

127   Blaise Pascal, *Pensées* (New York: Penguin Classics, 1995).

help to have a general understanding of some of the most common behavioral biases.

A complete list of the ways we are prone to irrationality would fill many volumes, but Kahneman and others identify the following innate biases investors should keep in mind:[128]

- *Attribute substitution.* This occurs when we face a complex question we can't answer, substitute a simpler question we can, and then fail to recognize our sleight of hand.

- *Confirmation bias.* This refers to the tendency to seek and interpret new evidence, not impartially but as validating of our preexisting beliefs or theories. As a result you can become entrenched in a bad decision despite objective evidence that you need to change. The familiar can become comfortable even if it's harmful.

- *Availability bias.* This occurs when we take a mental shortcut by prematurely making a decision on partial but readily available information—as if whatever we see or know is sufficient to make a rational choice. For investors, a steady stream of readily available but one-sided doom or elation on television and in news sources can lead to irrational decisions.

- *Hindsight bias.* This is the tendency to look back on an event as if it were predictable when, in fact, it was not. Kahneman says it allows us to maintain a comforting but falsely simple worldview. Why is that a problem? Because "it blinds us to surprises, it prevents us from learning the right thing; it allows us to learn the wrong thing: whenever we're surprised

---

128 In addition to the works cited above by Kahneman, Crosby, and Richards, see "Six Cognitive Biases, Heuristics, and Illusions That Daniel Kahneman Thinks Investors Should Know," *Vintage Value Investing*, January 20, 2020.

by something, even if we do admit that we've made a mistake we say, 'I'll never make that error again.' But in fact what you should learn when you make a mistake (because you did not anticipate something) is that the world is difficult to anticipate. That's the correct lesson to learn from surprises. That the world is surprising. It's not that my prediction is wrong. It's that predicting in general is almost impossible."

- *Anchoring bias.* This occurs when the first information we gain on a topic falsely colors all subsequent information.

- *Loss aversion bias.* This is an evolutionary adaptation that encourages us to take immediate and often drastic action when threatened with any kind of loss. That may make sense when our ancient ancestors relocated at the first sign of a grizzly bear near their tribal hunting ground, but it's ill-suited to modern investors who respond to any dip in the market by selling all their stocks. A rational investor must find ways to short-circuit our hard-wired but no-longer-adaptive response to the slightest threat of loss.

One of the best ways to avoid these pitfalls is to work with an advisor or a coach who can act as emotional circuit breakers by circumventing your tendencies to chase returns or run for cover in emotionally charged markets. In the process a good advisor may prevent significant wealth destruction and add significantly to your lifetime investment returns. A single such intervention could offset years of an advisor's fees.

At a minimum, develop a rules-based approach and an awareness of the behavioral biases discussed above. However, be realistic about the benefits of this education. Nobel Prize–winning behavioral economist Daniel Kahneman once stated that even though studying these errors was his life's work, he still falls prey to them.

Why Values Matter

First of all, if you identify mistakes you made in the past or areas where you've invested emotionally instead of rationally, congratulations! You are human! As a matter of fact, financial professionals are subject to making these same behavioral mistakes. Second, if we are interested in achieving what Mitch Anthony calls "return on life" as much as "return on investment," we may sometimes want to make an "irrational" decision we feel good about, provided we've done the analytical thinking up front and understand the trade-offs.

Finance textbooks are full of theory, utility curves, and the search for rational investors. In the real world, however, we make trade-offs and judgments that may be mathematically and financially suboptimal but are still good decisions for us. For instance, with a given risk tolerance and mortgage interest rate, I could mathematically demonstrate that having a mortgage and investing your cash would result in more wealth. This is a rational decision. However, the peace of mind, the freedom, and the biblical admonition that the borrower is servant to the lender may trump this option for you.

I once had a client who was planning on leaving a high-paying job at a major corporation and using part of his qualified retirement plan to start a ministry. His financial future—and that of his family—was at risk by this "irrational" decision. But both he and his wife trusted that this was their calling and understood the potential consequences. Therefore, I wholeheartedly supported their choice. My advice is that you be conscious of your values and recognize that sometimes the financially rational decision is not the best one for you. A holistic advisor can help you evaluate these trade-offs.

Why I'm a Rational Optimist

Despite being a realist about our inborn penchant for irrationality, I'm still what Matt Ridley calls a "rational optimist"[129] about our collective future. Those glued to their news feeds may think the world is getting worse, but that emotionally skewed view simply doesn't align with reality. As Harvard professor Steven Pinker points out, "Though the availability bias hides it from us, human progress is an empirical fact. When we look beyond the headlines to the trend lines, we find that humanity overall is healthier, richer, longer-lived, better fed, better educated, and safer from war, murder, and accidents than in decades and centuries past."[130] Ridley concurs, "The availability of almost everything a person could want or need has been going rapidly upward for 200 years and erratically upward for 10,000 years."

Still skeptical? Consider the following small sample of the generally overlooked (and always underreported) specifics from Ronald Bailey and Marian L. Tupy:[131]

According to the World Bank, 42 percent of the globe's population was still living in absolute poverty in 1981. In 2020, that figure was 8.65 percent, and it continues to decline. That's a decrease of roughly 80 percent.

---

129 Matt Ridley, *The Rational Optimist: How Prosperity Evolves* (New York: Harper Collins e-books, 2010).

130 Steven Pinker, *Rationality: What It Is, Why It Seems Scarce, Why It Matters* (New York: Viking, 2021).

131 Ronald Bailey and Marian L. Tupy, *Ten Global Trends Every Smart Person Should Know: And Many Others You Will Find Interesting* (Washington, DC: Cato Institute, 2020).

Since 1820, the size of the world's economy has grown more than a hundredfold.

Agricultural productivity has improved 60 percent since 1940 because of more scientific methods of farming, access to plentiful and much improved fertilizers and pesticides, and new high-yield and disease-resistant plants.

The global tree canopy increased by 865,000 square miles between 1982 and 2016.

And to critics such as Peter Thiel who suggest that technological innovation and advances have stagnated, a discerning public might counter that "the COVID-19 vaccines are the fastest ever created. In a remarkable achievement of medical science, we've gone from identifying a new pathogen … to discovering an immune response against it to developing and testing a safe and effective vaccine in less than 12 months. Previously, the fastest vaccine to go from development to deployment was the mumps vaccine in the 1960s, which took about four years."[132]

Of course, none of this is to suggest that we no longer face significant problems and challenges—or to minimize the suffering of those who have not reaped the benefits of the advances I've just cited. But details like these should provide a hopeful counterweight to the negativity and the scarcity mindset that pervade the 2020s.

Whatever our ongoing problems and challenges, whatever work remains to be done, that so many of us can plan for any kind of second act—much less the exciting, rewarding, and spiritually meaningful one I've described throughout the book—indicates that rational optimism, not anti-logical pessimism, ought to be the dominant philosophical spirit of our age. As a Christian, I'm under no delusions about human perfectibility or our chances of creating heaven on earth.

---

132 Sandy Cohen, "The fastest vaccine in history," UCLA Health, December 10, 2020.

But neither do I side with today's fashionable dystopian philosophers who cynically reject progress as a delusion.[133] By any yardstick, the world is improving, and anyone reading this book is well-positioned to contribute to that ongoing improvement.

As we turn to our conclusion and call to action, keep in mind the rhetorical question, posed in 1830, by the British historian and essayist Thomas Babington Macaulay about those nostalgic doomsayers, present in every age, convinced that society had reached a dire turning point and that its best days were in the past: "On what principle is it that when we see nothing but improvement behind us, we are to expect nothing but deterioration before us?"[134]

I hope the hero's path we've explored in the previous fifteen chapters has encouraged you to see your second, third, fourth, and fifth acts as stages on which your new financial clarity enables you to replace the illogical pessimism Macauley decries with the life of meaning and purpose you deserve.

---

133 See, for example, the British philosopher John Gray, particularly *The Silence of Animals: On Progress and Other Modern Myths* (New York: Penguin, 2013).

134 Thomas Babington Macaulay, "Southey's Colloquies on Society," *Edinburgh Review*, 1930 (https://www.econlib.org/library/Essays/macS.html).

Conclusion

I began this book with a difficult story to share about my father. Like Job in the Bible, he has dealt with many challenges. But like the heroes of great stories who pass through their trials and reach their happy conclusions, my father is "finishing well." He found purpose in taking care of my mother, being a sage and mentor to the next generation at the bank, and being the leader to our growing family. He remains a model for me every day.

Books often close with a call to action: authors impart what they hope is wisdom and ask the reader to go forth and apply it to some specific challenge according to a prescribed methodology. That works great if the goal involves mastering a common set of skills on the way to an identical objective (e.g., gardening, playing the piano, hiking the Appalachian Trail, removing an appendix).

But this book allows no such uniform summary formula, nor can I tell you, "Now put down the book and do X, Y, and Z." Identifying your life's unique deeper purpose, setting forth on your specific Act 2 journey, ensuring you have the financial means to pursue your individual dreams—these all involve moments of self-discovery, and concluding with an injunction to "discover yourself" would be laughingly inadequate. Each of the selves we discover will differ; each of our journeys and destinations will be distinct.

As Walt Whitman said, "Not I, nor anyone else can travel that road for you. You must travel it by yourself." Speaking as your guide at this parting crossroad, I cannot assure you precisely what challenges and joys you'll find on the unblazed trail ahead, but I want to leave you with the assurance that your second, third, fourth, and fifth acts can be—as in Shakespeare's plays—the best parts of your life's drama.

That I can't provide a one-size-fits-all call to action doesn't mean you don't have to act. But you'll need to define what that action is. So take what you've read and go to the woods (or wherever you do your best thinking) and contemplate or pray until you find out what makes your heart come alive. Once you've done that, use the resources I've provided to plan both your heart's journey and the financial steps that allow you to fulfill your version of a meaningful life.

And at that point, you must act, not according to my ideals but according to your own. This will take courage. You may need to consult a guide. But as I've said, the best plan or process in the world is useless unless you put it into practice. Moreover, don't paralyze yourself by being afraid to fail. The world and your heart will give you feedback, and you can adjust your plan accordingly. That freedom is what makes this stage of your life so exciting and rewarding. Ultimately the whole purpose of this book is to enable you to relax, surrender to God, and live your life with joy—as you uniquely define it.

In my thirty-six years as a financial advisor, I've realized that true wealth is made up of things money can't buy and death can't take away. I believe we were all created for a purpose, and I believe that sound financial planning is a means to an end: it helps us create the freedom to become all that we were uniquely created for. As stated previously,

I became passionate about using our wealth management practice to help others create the capacity to pursue their ideals.

When I started writing, I had modest goals: to produce a book I could be proud of and that could help you, the hero in my story, to create the clarity and confidence to live a great life—as you define it. Earlier, I've described the qualities you should look for in a financial advisor. Across the country, first-rate candidates abound to fill these roles. I encourage you to seek out this help. If anything I have written in the book piques your interest in learning more about our unique process for helping you create clarity and confidence in your life, I would love to hear from you. You can email us at hello@jeffbernier-author.com or use the following contact information:

TandemGrowth Advisors, LLC
3820 Mansell Rd Suite T30, Alpharetta, GA 30022
770-641-6360
www.tandemgrowth.com/

Finally, I make no claim to the originality of the wide-ranging ideas I've presented. This book is a compilation of ideas and resources I have found valuable over my career. Please visit www.jeffbernierau-thor.com to subscribe to my blog, learn more, and review a resources page with books and other resources that I recommend to readers interested in digging deeper into the topics I've explored.

Acknowledgments

This book is a summary collection of many insights I have gained through thirty-six years as a wealth advisor and my journey to my own second act. Many people have influenced me over the course of these years. Their fingerprints are all over this book. As this book is launched into the world, I wish to disclose fully that most of the ideas, concepts, and strategies contained came from years of learning, research, life experience, client experiences, coaching, and great books.

As I mentioned in the dedication, my parents have had a huge influence on the person I am today—at least the good parts!

My wife, Ashley, rescued me in my young adult years, helped me to reconnect with my faith, and continues to support me in my second act.

The TandemGrowth team—specifically Mona Fahmy, Jamie Stolz, and Cheryl Teal—has allowed me to focus on my unique gifts and to pursue those activities that I find fascinating and motivating, while continuing to manage their everyday responsibilities to our clients. Their efforts allowed me the time I needed to dedicate to this book.

The TandemGrowth client families: It is a great privilege to partner with and serve our clients. I find great meaning in helping these families pursue their visions. Their dreams, plans, and challenges motivated me to share the information in this book. I learn from our clients every day.

The Halftime Institute taught me a lot of concepts that I developed further in this book. Bob Buford's book, *Halftime*, and the Halftime Institute's workshop experience helped me go "from success to significance" in the second half.

Dick Gygi partnered with me as my Halftime coach. His wisdom and encouragement helped me see a bigger purpose for my work and how we serve clients.

Larry Maddox, Kevin Korhorn, Rob Hoxton, and I have enjoyed a twenty-five-year relationship in a best practices study group. Their influence on both my professional and my personal life is immeasurable.

Dan Sullivan and the Strategic Coach Program material helped me to uncover my Unique Ability® and learn how to be an entrepreneur.

The National Christian Foundation helped me learn ways to give in the most effective way.

The team and resources from Dimensional Fund Advisors were instrumental in helping with graphics, statistics, and information related to evidence-based investing.

There are many financial writers and consultants whose influence you will find in this book. While this list is not exhaustive, a few whose writings were particularly helpful are Nick Murray, Mitch Anthony, Daniel Crosby, and Larry Swedroe.

The many books and writings of Franciscan friar and teacher Richard Rohr also had a considerable influence on portions of this book.

Tim McBride with Advantage Media was a wonderful collaborator in helping me develop and improve the ideas in this book. I appreciate his commitment to this project.

About the Author

Jeff Bernier is a Certified Financial Planner® professional, public speaker, and author with more than thirty-six years of experience providing personalized financial planning advice to individuals and families. As president and founder of TandemGrowth Financial Advisors, LLC, a fee-only wealth management firm, his mission is to help people create the clarity and confidence to lead a great life—as they uniquely define it.

Jeff believes we are all uniquely created by God with a purpose, and his work focuses on helping others merge their financial resources with their inner lives, their spiritual quests with their material needs, and their money with life's true meaning. He is passionate about sharing the money and meaning message—how to apply academic research to build sound investment portfolios (evidence-based investing) and provide perspective to encourage healthy investor behavior.

Jeff is a husband, father, and grandfather. He enjoys playing golf, fishing, traveling, and reading. He uses his life experience and his professional knowledge to help others explore how wealth and joy can grow together in every phase of life.

Learn More about Jeff

No matter what stage of the financial journey you are in, visit Jeff to learn how you can incorporate meaning or to book him to speak at your next event:

www.jeffbernierauthor.com   hello@jeffbernierauthor.com

Work with Jeff

A passionate team of collaborators stands ready to partner with you at

TandemGrowth Financial Advisors

www.tandemgrowth.com

770.641.6360 info@tandemgrowth.com

3820 Mansell Road, Suite T30

Alpharetta, Georgia 30022

The Money and Meaning Show Podcast

Join Jeff each month as he shares insights and real-world strategies to help you gain the confidence and freedom to live a life of personal significance.

Listen in on Spotify, Amazon Music, or Apple Podcast.

Legal Stuff

Jeff Bernier is an investment advisor representative of TandemGrowth Financial Advisors, LLC, ("TandemGrowth") an investment advisor registered with the US Securities and Exchange Commission. Registration as an investment advisor is not an endorsement by securities regulators and does not imply that TandemGrowth has attained a certain level of skill, training, or ability. No person will receive cash or non-cash compensation, directly or indirectly, in exchange for an endorsement of this book. Any endorsement of the book *The Money and Meaning Journey* are endorsements of the book and are not endorsements of Jeff Bernier's reputation or experience as an investment advisor representative of TandemGrowth, or of TandemGrowth itself. The information presented in this book is general commentary intended to inform its readers, including current and prospective investors, about the broader financial ecosystem. Except for this contact page, this book is not intended as an offer of Mr. Bernier's or TandemGrowth's advisory services related to the sale or recommendation of securities. Not all services will be appropriate or necessary for all clients, and the potential value and benefit of TandemGrowth's services will vary based upon the client's individual investment, financial, and tax circumstances. The effectiveness and potential success of a tax strategy, investment strategy, and financial plan depend on a variety of factors, including but not limited to the manner and timing of implementation, coordination with the client and the client's other engaged professionals, and market conditions. Past performance does not guarantee future results. All investment strategies have the potential for profit or loss, and different investments and types of investments involve varying degrees of risk. There can be no assurance that the future performance of any specific investment or investment strategy, including those undertaken or recommended by TandemGrowth, will be profitable or equal any historical performance level. Additional information about TandemGrowth, including its Form ADV Part 2A describing its services, fees, and applicable conflicts of interest and its Form CRS, is available upon request and currently at https://adviserinfo.sec.gov/firm/summary/125490.